Coastal gardening

Coastal gardening

JOHN BICKERTON

AND

GRAHAM CLARKE

with special photography by
Andrea Jones

GUILD OF MASTER
CRAFTSMAN PUBLICATIONS

First published 2009 by
Guild of Master Craftsman Publications Ltd
Castle Place, 166 High Street,
Lewes, East Sussex BN7 1XU

Associate Publisher: Jonathan Bailey
Production Manager: Jim Bulley
Managing Editor: Gerrie Purcell
Senior Project Editor: Virginia Brehaut
Editor: Judith Chamberlain-Webber
Managing Art Editor: Gilda Pacitti
Designers: John Bickerton, Alison Walper

Set in Helvetica Neue and Zapfino

Colour origination by GMC Reprographics
Printed and bound by Kyodo Nation Printing, Thailand

Contents

ABOVE *Luxury by the sea in Santa Barbara, California, USA.*

Introduction

HAVING A PLACE NEAR TO THE COAST brings so much pleasure. If your property is close enough to the sea, you may have fine views and even be able to enjoy the soothing 'whoosh' of the waves as they lap against the beach – or 'crash' if the weather is more stormy. You do not have to move too far inland and away from the coastline to be able to take in the misty, salty air and enjoy the summer breezes, whereas further inland the air could be sultry and oppressive. For many, being by the coast brings a certain peace and tranquillity that is good for the soul. This is, after all, why so many people retire to the coast or choose to have second homes there. They can get away from it all and recharge their batteries.

For a keen gardener, a seaside property provides as many as challenges it does opportunities. A coastal garden can suffer high-tide flooding, for example. Or it could sit atop several feet of extremely free-draining sandy soil which lacks goodness, does not retain moisture, and becomes scorching hot in summer. Or the garden could bathe in harsh sunlight that turns the most delicate plants to a crisp.

The two most important issues facing a coastal garden are wind and salt. Wind can collect out at sea, gather some speed as it surges towards land, then charge through your coastal garden, leaving near devastation in its wake. This can be a regular occurrence. In many cases, as it hurls and twirls out at sea it whips up salty spray and, like a puppy bringing a stick, it carries the spray onto the shoreline, which results in a deposit of sea salt all over our gardens. This salt is certainly detrimental

to the long-term wellbeing of wood and metal items in the garden, but it can be deadly to plants – or at least some plants.

This is the key thing. You must know which plants to grow in your coastal garden. You must know how to integrate them to best advantage, and how to grow and maintain them. Your taste in plants and colour schemes will change and evolve over the years, and should you ever move to a second seaside property you can delight in growing an entirely different range of plants. We say this with confidence for, as you will discover later in this book, there are so many excellent seaside plants from which to choose.

As joint authors of this book we hope it will be as useful to you as it is beautiful. Our aim is to tell you and show you which flowers, trees, shrubs, vegetables and fruits will thrive in gardens that are

close to the sea. You will see how they work in established gardens, and there are plans for you to follow or adapt in your own coastal havens.

We have both been around long enough to have travelled extensively, and in our global trottings we have seen many hundreds of seaside and coastal gardens which are all paradises on Earth. Some were large private estates with magnificent views, whilst others were tiny courtyards. Some were entirely exposed to the elements, whilst others were sheltered enough to grow exotic plants. This book is a collection and a celebration of them. Thankfully our cameras were always working, and so we are delighted to show you just some of the wonderful seaside gardens we've seen. And to pass on some of the tips and advice picked up on the way.

John Bickerton & Graham Clarke

Part One

COASTAL
lifestyle

Modern-day living is not easy, with deadlines, targets, pressures, stresses and strains all taking their toll on people's quality of life, and for many of us it is just the thought of getting away from it all that enables us to deal with the difficulties of everyday life.

Chapter 1

WHY LIVE NEAR THE COAST?

A place by the sea as a main or second home can be many people's salvation. If the home comes with some land around it, this opens up a whole new realm of gardening possibilities as well as the opportunity for endless pleasure. People can change their lifestyle beyond measure.

RIGHT *A conservatory makes outdoor living by the coast a possibility all year round.*

Why choose the coast?

THERE IS REAL beauty on this planet of ours, but we can't always see it. Our professional and working lives often dominate and blind us to the natural wonders that are around us. However, if we take time out of our busy lives, we can see that we are surrounded by beautiful landscapes: scenic mountains and deep tree-lined valleys … golden deserts and jungles teeming with wildlife … rolling hills and shimmering lakes … and, of course, our coastal regions.

In many places, the coastline forms the most awe-inspiring of all of earth's natural phenomena and, incredibly, there are some 461,078 miles (742,000km) of land-based coastlines across the world. It is impossible to even guess at the number of people living in coastal regions – but it is believed that the majority of the world's population lives within 37 miles (60km) of the sea.

Historically, this may be because the sea offers a source of food and for reasons of economy. In more recent times, however, this mass migration coastwards has also been for the sake of wellbeing and to take advantage of a 'better' way of life.

The weather is regarded by most people as being more pleasant by the sea. In truth, it can be very similar to prevailing conditions inland, but skies are generally more open and, with fresh breezes off the sea, bad weather can often clear more quickly and the sun's strength can be more intense. A hot summer's day in an inland city, or in the centre of a large landmass, can be unpleasantly humid and

ABOVE *Bay of Islands, New Zealand. Inland, the weather can be similar to that experienced by the coast.*

BELOW LEFT *Houses in coastal areas often have a unique architectural style.*

BELOW *Wild vegetation growing at the water's edge will indicate the types of plants you can grow in nearby gardens.*

unbearably hot. The land all around reflects and radiates the heat, exacerbating the effect, whilst the spaces between tall buildings can trap hot, dry air. On the coast, a sea breeze blows in, reducing humidity and although surface temperatures may remain as warm as inland, the effects are reduced by the breeze, making the whole experience much more pleasant.

The coastal climate also seems to cause an infinite variation of light and colours – it is for this reason that the area around St Ives on the north coast of the English county of Cornwall has become famous the world over for painting. The sunlight here, if you believe the artists and the tourist offices, is Mediterranean-like. For some unexplained reason, it does actually seem brighter here, with cleaner, crisper air.

BETTER HEALTH

In Victorian England in the late nineteenth century, it was believed that being near to the sea was conducive to better health. A common phrase was to go to the seaside to 'convalesce'. Following an illness, or surgery, your constitution would, it was believed, be improved greatly by staying for a time by the sea. The belief was not always reliant on visiting a warm place either. For example, the town of Rothesay on the Scottish island of Bute still to this day evokes that Victorian era.

The Victorians put down the healthy, bracing air and distinctive smell of the seaside to ozone, but in fact the smell is not ozone (which would be extremely harmful). Instead, University of East Anglia (Norwich, UK) scientists have found the smell comes from dimethyl sulphide, which in high concentrations can irritate the eyes and lungs. Regardless of this piece of science, the belief has been perpetuated in the years since.

It is also worth pointing out the merits of cleaner coastal air over inland city air, and this really comes down to one word: pollution. Cities such as Pittsburgh – some 292 miles (470km) from the Atlantic Ocean – and Washington DC – some 62 miles (100km) from the same ocean – rank highly in the list of most polluted of US cities.

Of course, it depends on the type of heavy industry that takes place within the city, and perhaps it is unfair to highlight just two cities like this. However, it cannot be coincidence that most of the world's 10 worst polluted cities (in a report compiled over seven years by the Blacksmith Institute, a team of environmental and health experts) are inland. These include the Russian Federation cities of Dzherzhinsk, some 745 miles (1,200km) from the Caspian Sea; Norilsk, 217 miles (350km) from the Cara Sea; Linfen in China, 434 miles (700km) from the Yellow Sea; and, the most land-locked of all, Mayluu-Suu, Kyrgyzstan, 1,118 miles (1,800km) from the Caspian Sea.

RIGHT Reeds and grasses are tough enough to survive even the most exposed of positions close to the sea.

BELOW As coastal lifestyles have changed from traditional fishing to tourism, a now derelict trawler in Brixham, Devon UK, has been naturalised by a Buddleja.

A SECOND HOME

More affluent members of society often choose to own a second home. This can be part of a sound financial strategy, such as a long-term plan for retirement, and it can also provide them with valuable lifestyle options. Here are the four main reasons people buy a second home:

Sound investment

The housing market may go up and down, but in the long run it generally appreciates in value. As cities become more and more crowded, beautiful homes in beautiful settings will become increasingly rare – and valuable.

Rental opportunity

As housing and estate agents say: 'Pick a home you love and others will love it too.' When you own a second home, you open up the possibility of renting it out to others, which helps to pay off the mortgage at the same time.

Fun times

Perhaps the best way to use a second property is recreationally. If you love to fish, sail, water-ski or just walk along the shore, a home near the coast will be just the thing. Even when you love your main place of residence inland, being able to get away for a while is a great bonus.

Live by the coast and rent out your inland home

Many have successfully swapped their lives in the city for living by the sea. Technology has made it possible for many of us to work wherever we want, so why not take advantage of it and live where you want to? A move to a less populated area does not have to be prohibitively expensive nor does it have to be for ever. Instead of renting out your holiday home and living in the city, you can do the reverse. Urban homes are easier to rent out no matter what time of year it is, and the sense of wellbeing generated by this strategy is that you can feel like you're on holiday every day!

ABOVE *With gardens facing the open sea, many different types of plants can be grown.*

BELOW LEFT
Traditional seaside towns usually started off as ports or fishing harbours, as here in Brixham, Devon, UK.

DOWNSIZING AND RETIREMENT

Whether or not you own a second home, purchasing a property in an idyllic spot of your choice enables you to use it for your pleasure during your working life or as an additional income-generator. When it comes to retiring, you have the option of kicking off your shoes and permanently relocating to your second home, or even selling it and upgrading to another home in the same area.

Living by the coast can engender contentment and feelings of good health, and these are exactly the attributes sought by those planning to retire. Children have by now grown up and flown the nest, so this move to the coast frequently goes hand in hand with opting for a smaller property. It is a real lifestyle change for most people and something that is usually very welcome after years of working. It is a chance to wind down.

ENTERTAINING

Entertaining people by the sea is a world apart from entertaining inland. For a start, anyone who has grown up in a place a long way from the sea, and who then subsequently moves close to the sea, will know that their land-locked family and friends do like to come and stay – and often very regularly.

Entertaining may simply involve a meal outdoors or a garden barbecue. A coastal setting – and, even better, one with a view of the sea – will generally have a very different ambience to one inland or in a built-up environment.

Entertaining outdoors also gives you the opportunity to show your visitors your coastal garden – and your coastal gardening prowess. You will be able to demonstrate just what can be achieved near to the sea … and, if you choose the timing carefully, key plants in the garden will be at their best.

ABOVE Entertaining by the sea (in this instance, a wedding reception) can be a memorable experience.

BELOW A simple wooden deck and chair for relaxing can be entirely in keeping with a coastal garden.

LEFT Owning a property by the sea, especially if it has sea views, will make you feel as if you are on holiday all the time.

Where to go

WHERE SHOULD YOU LOOK for your spot near the sea? Those who are planning to buy a second home near the coast, or maybe even move permanently to a place on the coast, need to decide exactly where this should be.

In many cases the decision will be dictated by family connections to the area. It could be where someone came from originally and now they wish to return there to spend their remaining years. Or perhaps the destination may be chosen because it is somewhere that had previously been much enjoyed on holidays.

Occasionally, it has been known for people to choose a location because it offers the right climate, facilities, landscape, transport links and so on … yet they have never been there before, or not for any serious length of time. This may seem a rash move, but usually there will be a unique or dominating attribute that surpasses any other objections to the move. The reputation of the location could just be too enticing!

Coastal properties have appreciated at an average of 7 per cent annually over the past 50 years (according to a US federal study). A waterfront property is worth from 8 per cent to 45 per cent more than a comparable inland site.

But, let's face it, these prices can make the decision to move prohibitive to many people, and the supply of ideal places to live on the coast is limited. Unfortunately, unregulated development has marred the beauty of some areas; in others the economy is too closely tied to tourism to be able to support the good life all the year round. Perhaps there's too much visitor traffic in summer or there are too many storms in winter. There are, however, a few rules to follow to help you make up your mind whether to move coastwards.

ABOVE *Properties high above the water are unlikely to suffer from flooding, but beware of erosion.*

LEFT *Sheltered bays, such as this one in Kalkan, southern Turkey, will be better for plants that tolerate salty air, but dislike windy conditions.*

New builds

If you have bought a plot of land for building your own property, make sure that you ask local authorities about height limits, setbacks and wind-resistance rules. Learn the environmental laws; for example, you may be restricted in what you can build in areas that contain protected wildlife.

Coastal homes need to withstand the elements, which often means stronger (and more expensive) building materials, as well as specific design elements such as rounded rather than angular corners. Restrictions on sewage systems and septic tanks may dictate the size of the house that you can build. Having to transport heavy machinery and materials to an island or remote waterfront location will add to costs.

Public or private beaches

If you are buying a place partly because of its proximity to the beach, check whether the beach is public or private. If it is a public beach you will be powerless to stop people from setting up umbrellas and lounge chairs, spoiling the outlook for you.

Plan for insurance

It is important that you build sizeable insurance premiums into your budget. Some insurers have stopped insuring properties in coastal areas because of storm losses, so expect to pay more for less coverage. You could also need flood insurance. And be aware that insurers generally won't compensate you for land lost to beach erosion.

Plan for maintenance

Finally, remember that salt air is tough on homes and gardens, as well as cars, metal, wood, fabrics – in fact, anything left outdoors. If you live within a quarter of a mile of the beach, every time you throw open those French windows salt spray and mildew get inside the home; expect to replace rugs, appliances and even mirrors more often.

PRE-PURCHASE CHECKLIST

It is wise to analyse the wording in any sales documents properly. For example, 'ocean view' or 'sea view' does not necessarily mean the same thing as 'fronting on to the water'. Some people have purchased what they thought was a dream home near the beach, only to find some weeks later that there are bulldozers tearing up the ground between them and the sea for the development of a house that really will be 'fronting on to the water'.

Check for erosion and storm damage

Houses that have never been flooded and those with a sea wall are worth more than unprotected properties. Two other factors affecting property value are the distance of the house from the water and how frequently the beach undergoes a programme of renourishment. If you're purchasing an older home, have a structural engineer determine how vulnerable it is to storm damage. Then, no matter how old the construction, have your home inspected regularly for signs of corrosion.

LEFT *Lulworth Cove, on the World Heritage Jurassic Coastline, Dorset, UK, is a beautiful rural setting.*

COASTAL CITIES

Anyone choosing to live in a coastal city, such as Liverpool in the UK, Los Angeles in the USA, Vancouver in Canada, Sydney in Australia, and so on, will not just have to worry about the effects of salt and sand in the air. They will also need to address issues of pollution, as well as microclimates brought about by urban density. A plant that is tolerant of all these coastal and city-based problems, yet is a worthy subject for the garden, is a rare and valuable commodity!

Australia is, not surprisingly when you think about it, the country that boasts most cities on the coast. It is, after all, essentially one massive island, of which just the outer edge is really habitable – the inner, major portion being mainly desert and scrub.

Over 30 of Australia's key cities such as Sydney, Adelaide, Wollongong, Melbourne, Brisbane and Darwin are coastal, which means that more than 90 per cent of Australians live within a short distance of the sea.

A RURAL SETTING

Those moving out from large towns or cities will perhaps be looking for a complete change. The coast will, in the main, give them this change. But there is also the 'rural' element to bear in mind.

Most coastlines are narrow strips of land that are backed by several miles of countryside. There are almost certainly a few hamlets, villages and towns dotted about, but between them are many square miles of open countryside. This can be the ideal place if you want to 'get away from it all' or 'get closer to nature'. However, remote rural areas do not always offer a daily postal service – or express pick-up if you are running a business. It is important therefore to investigate these essential services before you move. You will also have less access to shops, although good internet access may solve this for you.

FOREIGN PARTS

It takes a pioneering sort of spirit to pack up and leave the country of your origin to live and, perhaps, work in another country, but it is happening more and more. Most of the items listed under Pre-purchase checklist (see page 19) will also apply to buying a coastal property abroad, but additional points to consider prior to making a foreign purchase include:

Language

Nothing will make you feel less at home than not being able to communicate. Going on a basic language course can have a very positive effect on your relocation experience. It will make the difference between being understood and feeling frustrated because no one knows what you are talking about.

Healthcare

Check what the healthcare facilities are in the country and locality of the new property. You should also confirm your cover with your medical insurance provider if you have one.

Paperwork

Make sure that all the necessary paperwork has been completed well in advance of your departure date. This will ensure that you do not have any last-minute panics about visas, insurance etc.

Keeping in touch

Leaving your friends and family is often the hardest thing about relocating abroad. Don't forget to give everyone that you want to keep in touch with your email address and telephone number before you go. Also you should remember to arrange for the redirection of your post after you have left so that you do not miss anything important.

Most of the world's coastal cities started as small shipping ports, and these sites were chosen because of deep-water channels and/or freshwater river estuaries. In many cases these cities are today the cause of much environmental concern, for one of the most challenging issues facing our oceans now is that of increasingly rapid coastal urbanization. With the majority of the world's population living within 37 miles (60km) of the coastline, and this figure steadily increasing, it is important that environmentalists assess the full implications of this urbanization.

Coastal ecosystems are amongst the most productive on earth, for some 90 per cent of the planet's living and non-living resources are found within a few hundred kilometres of the coast.

These valuable natural assets are seriously threatened by coastal sprawl and pollution. Climate change means that there are additional coastal threats too, including rising sea levels, and the ever-present danger of extreme events such as tropical storms and tsunamis.

Living in a coastal city brings with it a number of personal, environmental and economic pressures, but, given the space, you can still create the idyllic garden of your dreams.

ABOVE *The skyline of Halifax, Nova Scotia. This busy and bustling city boasts many fine gardens, but is regularly battered by salty – and cold – winds.*

BELOW *With a population of some three million people, the city of Auckland, New Zealand, is entirely coastal in nature.*

Chapter 2

THE CHALLENGES OF COASTAL GARDENING

 We have seen why people like to live near to the sea, but enjoying this way of life does not come without its problems. Gardeners, particularly, must account for the vagaries of the climate, and it is not unheard of for people to move to the coast, find it is not to their liking, then move back inland. This chapter is designed to alert you to the problems before you make your decision to move seawards.

RIGHT *Many gardens with beautiful views, such as this one at Newlyn in Cornwall, UK, can be exposed, so be careful where you place your seating.*

Wind

THE ASPECT OF THE weather that tends to affect the lifestyle of coastal dwellers the most is the wind. In meteorological terms, there are two basic types of wind you will find at the coast:

• A 'pressure wind' – created by air movements from high and low pressures. There are four basic pressure types: anticyclone, ridge of high pressure, depression and trough of low pressure.
• A sea (or 'onshore') breeze – this blows from the cool sea surface on to land, where the air is warming and rising during the day. By mid-afternoon, a sea breeze can spread as much as 15–30 miles (24–48km) inland. At night sometimes the reverse can happen; the land cools and the sea can be warmer, so air travels from the land and towards the sea (known as an 'offshore' breeze).

Coastal wind speed depends on the sea breeze and the pressure wind. Wind near the coast is stronger than elsewhere if the two components act together in the same direction, but is less if the two components oppose each other.

A sea breeze, bringing cold air inland, may confront an area of warmer air over the land which is moving in the opposite direction. A roll of shallow cloud often forms at the junction, which is known as a 'sea breeze front'.

WIND PROTECTION

Shelter is essentially provided by vertical structures, and these fall into three different categories – walls, fences, and natural screens and hedges – with a number of subcategories.

Walls

There are two types of stone wall. A 'dry-stone wall' is made without mortar and is usually well suited to rural and coastal situations. The other type is the mortared stone wall, which is stronger and able usually to retain soil, at least for part of the way up. These mortared walls do not look as rustic, but they can be made to look more like a dry-stone wall by 'raking' out the joints.

Brick and block walls are more commonly used for buildings than garden features or boundaries, but they can be very effective in a decorative sense. Block walls, which are much cheaper to build than brick walls, are usually rendered to produce a surface that is smooth and attractive, which can then be painted.

The only problem with having a rendered wall close to the sea is that the constant buffeting by wind – and the inevitable salty corrosion – means that the rendered surface can crack and peel. Scraping, filling, smoothing and painting may be necessary every one or two years, depending on the age of the wall and the prevailing conditions.

Screen-block walls became very popular in the 1970s, and they have never really gone away since. These 'see-through' patterned blocks are attractive and useful, but they produce a weak wall in comparison to solid brick, block or stone, and for this reason a screen-block wall should be strengthened with several supporting piers.

BELOW *A solid stone wall is usually in keeping with a coastal or rustic setting.*

ABOVE FAR LEFT *A decorative 'wall' made from roof tiles.*

ABOVE LEFT AND CENTRE *Chestnut fencing or 'paling', close-bonded and open.*

ABOVE *Secure horizontal wooden slat fencing with stout wooden posts will last for years.*

Fences

A fence is not going to be as durable as a properly built wall, but you may decide to choose a fence for financial reasons or because, aesthetically, a fence is more appropriate to the garden.

Timber panel fencing is the most common type. This could be overlapping horizontal larch strips, interwoven strips, or close-boarded fencing using vertical feather-edged boards. These panels are joined together via stout wooden or concrete posts; the former may last just a few years in a very exposed coastal situation, whereas the latter should last for many years.

Metal fencing is commonplace too. Wire fences include chain link, chicken wire and 'livestock' fencing. There are also steel fences in the form of decorative wrought iron and vertical railings. These last two are expensive in comparison, but can look magnificent in the right setting. Be aware, however, that metal corrodes and rusts much more quickly where there is salt in the air, so be prepared for high annual maintenance.

LEFT *This tree on Guernsey has been affected by constant wind battering. The 'lean' is caused by the wind drying out the growth buds.*

Natural screens

These are panels made from woven willow and hazel (known as 'hurdles'), or bamboo, reed and sometimes even heather. Split bamboo screens also come in rolls. In all cases the panels are wired to rustic posts, and they make quick, easy and relatively cheap screens. However, they are nowhere near as permanent as the other types of fences mentioned, nor as durable.

WINDBREAKS AND SHELTER BELTS

By far the best way of reducing the impact of the wind, if there is space, is to put up a windbreak to filter the wind.

An effective windbreak should be high; it is estimated that a windbreak 20ft (6m) high offers wind protection to a man standing 50ft (15m) away. Also, the denser the planting, the better the protection. Depending on the situation, even a low shrub border just 10ft (3m) high and comprising a variety of bushy plants can be effective. A windbreak should preferably comprise evergreen subjects so that there is year-round leaf cover, but deciduous trees and shrubs in their dormant season can still work very well at reducing wind speed.

Windbreaks are certainly better at reducing wind severity than solid walls and fences, as these can create turbulence and 'eddies' by forcing the wind up and over them, to descend again on the leeward side. Such turbulence can damage any plants that are within the vicinity.

ABOVE Tasmanian or Australian blackwood trees make a dense shelter belt.

RIGHT Tender plants such as cacti and succulents usually appreciate shelter, provided here (and below right) by bamboo screens.

BELOW A distant shelter belt of trees.

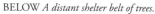

If you put up a wide band of trees and shrubs, two or more deep, then this is more often referred to as a 'shelter belt'. If substantial trees are your choice for a shelter belt, you should be prepared for a wait. In the mid-1800s Osgood Mackenzie, owner and founder of Inverewe in the north of Scotland set out a belt of the Monterey pine (*Pinus radiata*) – then left them for 25 years before planting his garden! However, it might take just a decade or so for a belt of year-old trees or saplings to develop into a useful shelter belt.

The following conifers, in addition to the Monterey pine, make fine subjects for shelter belts: the beach pine (*P. contorta)*, the lodgepole pine (*P. contorta latifolia*) and the Monterey cypress (*Cupressus macrocarpa*) – but the latter should be left unclipped, as it does not make a good trimmed hedge. The two best deciduous trees are ash (*Fraxinus excelsior*) and sycamore (*Acer pseudoplatanus*), although in the early years both may be slightly shaped by the wind.

Hedges

A gardener should always have at least one hedge to look after. Planting a hedge and maintaining it are both 'real' gardening jobs, requiring skill and insight. Painting fences with preservative, or wrought iron with rust preventative, is a do-it-yourself property maintenance job! Additionally, a mature hedge can look wonderful, filter the wind magnificently and be a haven for wildlife.

In the case of a coastal garden you will need to make sure that the plants chosen for the hedge are suitable for battering from wind and salt; if there is space, you may like to consider planting a shelter belt on the windward side of the hedge – this really will give you the best outlook horticulturally.

As for suitable plants, amongst the best are *Griselinia littoralis,* holly (*Ilex aquifolium*), evergreen oleaster (*Elaeagnus* x *ebbingei, E. pungens* and its variegated forms), *Escallonia, Olearia, Euonymus japonicus, Pittosporum* and *Brachyglottis.*

Anchoring furniture

In exposed gardens light items of furniture can be blown over – or across distances. It makes sense to anchor these down somehow, or to stack them and put them in storage if bad weather is forecast. Of course, the heavier the furniture is, the less movement there will be.

Many suites of garden furniture these days come with pre-made covers for use during off-season periods. If these covers are used, and they encompass, say, a table and its chairs, and the cover is firmly fixed in place, there is less likelihood of wind movement and the whole suite should be secure. However, it is always better to put furniture into winter storage, if this is available.

ABOVE LEFT *A trimmed formal hedge comprising sea buckthorn and* Hippophae rhamnoides.

ABOVE *A loose, less formal hedge consisting of* Pittosporum tobira.

RIGHT *A wide veranda is the perfect place to relax in the cool of the day and to take in your coastal views.*

GARDENS ON THE BEACH

Throughout this book we speak at length about the problems brought about by exposing plants – and gardens – to the wind, and also about the harmful effects of salt spray. Nowhere is this felt more keenly than when you garden right on the shoreline. In the flats of a river estuary, or in the dunes of a beach facing the prevailing wind, there will be so many obstacles to overcome it is only the dedicated and the brave who can create a worthy garden.

Only the toughest of plants will survive this situation. Choosing them carefully is critical, especially when you bear in mind that they should also be, at least in part, decorative.

There is a handful of such exposed beach gardens that have attracted worldwide acclaim, despite the disadvantages of their position. One such garden – that of the late film director Derek Jarman, at Dungeness in the county of Kent, southeast England – has attracted a degree of controversy as well. Is it a carefully crafted artist's garden full of hidden meaning and great depth? Or is it merely a selection of disparate plants and flotsam set out on a beach in a random way?

RIGHT AND BELOW *The garden of the late Derek Jarman is loved and loathed by gardening enthusiasts in equal measure.*

Prospect Cottage, Kent, UK

Since his death in 1994, filmmaker Derek Jarman has in some ways had his reputation as a director and painter eclipsed by the notoriety of his garden. His final, and some would say most improbable, incarnation was as a gardener. He kept diaries and made a film whereby he chronicled the creation of the garden at Prospect Cottage, an old fisherman's dwelling built of tarred timber. With the towering Dungeness power station as a backdrop, the garden was fashioned out of local materials, driftwood, beach pebbles, and plants able to survive the whipping wind and salt spray.

There are no boundaries or fences to the garden – just endless shingle beach. The environment is harsh: baking sun and drying winds in summer, with no shade to be had for miles in any direction, and in winter the sea storms are laced with salt water and, often, biting Siberian winds.

To be honest, there is not much planting to see, and you will not stay around long. However, the setting is stunning (see page 188 for details).

ABOVE *The area around the old fisherman's cottage is completely exposed, with no available shade – at any time of the year.*

PLAN: A BEACH GARDEN

By following this plan, a beach gardener would be able to re-create the kind of area Derek Jarman built around his fisherman's hut. Careful use of shingle and driftwood (or other scraps from the beach) can help to form the structural element to the garden. Low planting is required at the perimeter of the area, so as not to spoil views.

A   Shed
B   Deck and steps
C   Parking hard area
D   Planting for screening
E   Concentric rings/post
F   Shingle open space
G   Small size shingle
H   Wildlife pond
I   Scrap sculpture
J   Concentric rings
K   Planting for screening
L   Beach
M   Low planting

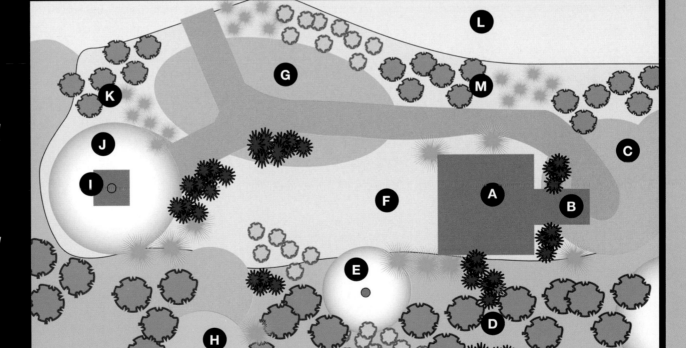

The beach garden

If you have an area on the beach, or set in shingle, and you want to re-create the sort of garden adored by Derek Jarman, you will not find it difficult. There is, after all, no hard landscaping to construct – it is there already, in the form of shingle or sand. You will not need to mark out areas for pathways, as there aren't any – you just walk between the plants.

Part of the pleasure of the garden at Prospect Cottage is the curious emerging purple shoots of sea kale (Crambe maritima) anchored deep in the moving shingle, with their long taproots. A maritime form of herb robert (Geranium robertianum) grows in a tight alpine dome and tolerates the entwining tendrils of a sea pea. Then there are the misty blue leaves of the yellow horned poppy (Glaucium flavum), and the dry, dead spires of last year's dock flowers.

To the front of Prospect Cottage there is a quite traditional cottage garden of circular, square and rectangular beds defined by upstanding flint stones. It is planted with lavenders, santolinas, poppies and sea kale.

LEFT *Sea kale* (Crambe maritima) *will happily grow in shingle.*

BELOW Agapanthus *and Californian poppies.*

BELOW RIGHT *Hawkbit thriving on a shingle beach.*

Walkways

If your property is – literally – on the beach (and it will more than likely be on a shingle beach, owing to the instability of sand), then you should construct a stable pathway across to the dwelling from the boundary. This will provide for wheeled access (prams, wheelchairs, wheelbarrows etc.) as well as giving the area a base for its design.

RIGHT *A beach or shingle garden at your own home needs to be thought about carefully, as sometimes they can look 'wild and rampant' when what you really want is 'natural and serene'.*

LEFT *Derek Jarman's house and garden are visited by thousands every year.*

The love of lavender

Thus far we have noted that Derek Jarman's garden is in a place called Dungeness, and that lavender has been planted in its front garden. This silvery green perennial sub-shrub, with its thick and sturdy stems and leaves, and its useful tolerance of dry, sandy soil, makes a fine plant for a beach garden.

Curiously, halfway across the world from Dungeness, UK, there is a certified organic lavender farm overlooking a place called Dungeness Bay, in the US state of Washington. Jardin du Soleil is located on the Olympic Peninsula, 4 miles (6.5km) north of the town of Sequim (see page 188 for details).

Planted in 1999 on land that was part of a dairy farm established in the 1880s, there are Victorian gardens, ponds and fruit trees. And lavender fields encompass the landscape with the Strait of Juan de Fuca beyond.

Thousands of lavender plants on more than 10 acres (4ha) create a wonderfully fragrant vista. The farm and gardens are open daily throughout summer; the plants are in bloom from the end of June through to August, with harvesting starting in July. Members of the public who go along can pick their own lavender bouquets or buy plants to grow at home.

The problems of salt

SEA WATER CONTAINS approximately 3 per cent salt as well as other minerals. However, the proportion varies considerably, according to the ground over or through which the water has been fed.

The sea with the highest salt content, and therefore the highest density, is the Dead Sea between Israel, the West Bank and Jordan. It is so named because nothing will live in it; normal saltwater fish species die as soon as they are put into it. It is actually a large inland lake, some 1,300ft (394m) below the level of the nearest open sea, the Mediterranean. It is the lowest stretch of water on the planet and contains about 25 per cent salts, of which 7 per cent is common salt. Understandably, no vegetation of garden merit grows along the banks of the Dead Sea; you would be hard-pressed even to find any highly salt-tolerant reeds and grasses.

Generally, sea water freezes at a lower temperature than fresh water, at between –1.5° and –2°C (29° and 28°F), depending on the degree of salinity. As it freezes it separates and becomes a mixture of freshwater ice, brine and air. Water just below sea ice may be more salty than the rest. Estuary water is a mixture of sea water and fresh river water and is therefore considerably less saline than open sea. Consequently, estuaries freeze more readily than the sea.

Salt-laden sea water causes problems for plants in two ways: salty air and seawater flooding. Let's take the most common of the problems first.

RIGHT *The Dead Sea in the Middle East is so strongly salty that very little vegetation grows there.*

ABOVE *Dunes are so sandy and salty that only the most tolerant and durable plants – mainly grasses – are able to grow there.*

TOP RIGHT *Salty air is created by the wind whipping up droplets of sea water and carrying them inland.*

RIGHT *The rare event of snowfall on the natural 'gateway' of Durdle Door on the UK's Dorset coastline.*

SALTY AIR

How does the air become salty? Out at sea, the wind will whip up droplets of water, and the smallest, finest ones are carried inland on air currents. As they travel inland, some of the water evaporates and this makes the remaining solution more salt-concentrated. These droplets can be held aloft for several miles before settling, and of course this may be on any surface, from soil and plants, to cars, buildings, animals … anything.

Unless washed away by rain, or water from a sprinkler or hose, the salt level will build up and this accumulation of deposit is, in the main, what causes damage to plants. The degree of salinity in the air varies hugely depending on four variables:

- The salinity level of the sea
- The wind speed and direction
- The mean air temperature
- The distance travelled.

As for this last variable, it has been recognized that salt spray is most damaging to plants growing within 1,000ft (305m) of the shoreline.

Coastal garden owners in some parts of the world, including the US Eastern Seaboard, are fortunate in that the worst of the storms come in late summer and autumn, when there is not so much in the way of new, emerging growth and buds to be damaged. But the news is not so good for gardeners in the south and west of England and Wales, and the west coasts of Scotland and Ireland,

as the westerly winds regularly batter gardens that have been brought on earlier by the flow of warm waters via the Gulf Stream.

Salt can also be deposited by sea mist and fog (see page 37) which closes in around plants. When the air is still, droplets of salty water settle on leaves and stems. The water evaporates when the mist clears, leaving a dry salty covering that remains in place until it is washed away by rain, or the gardener when watering plants.

Salty air is not always a bad thing. It is well known that salt spray rids certain plants of insect infestations (roses and hollies reportedly have less aphid presence in coastal gardens), and it also helps to control fungal diseases (zinnias and lilacs do not so readily succumb to mildew, to which they are usually prone).

ABOVE *Sea water is fine for cleansing seashells, but it will damage garden soil forever.*

SEA WATER IN THE SOIL

The two ways in which sea water gets into the soil are fairly rare but, if environmentalists are to be believed, they will become more common over the next 100 years or so.

The first and more obvious way is through seawater flooding. Unless your garden leads down to the tidal water's edge, this is unlikely to be a serious threat. But there are freak occasions when tides can flood a beach and flow through gaps in the dunes, dikes or levees, and even pour right over gardens farther inland. The gardens most affected will be those in the lowest lying areas. It is claimed that the incidences of storms and floods (and in extreme cases, hurricanes and cyclones) will increase and become more severe as a result of climate change, and this should be borne in mind by anyone wanting to embark on creating a coastal garden.

The second way for sea water to get into the soil is less visible. During a drought the water table can drop so low that sea water gets into the ground water. When ground water becomes salty, plants draw up the salt via their roots, and too much can cause a withdrawal of moisture from the leaves, a process known as 'exosmosis'. Plants become dehydrated and wilt (and eventually die).

Unfortunately the gardener usually thinks the problem is a lack of ground moisture, so applies more water to the soil. If this water is also salty, it just makes the problem worse.

Saline infiltration of ground water is becoming more problematic as the urbanization of seaside towns grows, which puts more pressure on finite water supplies.

SALT-TOLERANT PLANTS

The vast majority of plants recommended in this book will be tolerant of average salt-air levels. The only exceptions will be annuals, which last for just one or two growing seasons, and short-term vegetable crops, which do not stay in the garden long enough to suffer damage.

However, the more extreme the exposure to salty air, both in terms of the length of time of the exposure and the degree of salinity, the more damage there will be to the plants.

Typical damage will be a scorching of leaf margins, a powdery coating of salt on dry leaves, burnt tips to tender new growth in spring and, in severe and long-lasting cases, all of the above combined with a general wilting.

FAR LEFT *Virginia creeper* (Parthenocissus quinquefolia).

LEFT *African lily* (Agapanthus hybrid).

This damage is rarely to be found all over a plant, however. The side nearest the sea is likely to be in receipt of the most salt deposit, and growth on that side will slow down as the salt draws moisture from the plant's tissues – leaves, buds and stems. The side of the plant facing away from the sea will have less salt deposited on it and will continue to grow more or less normally. Eventually the plant will become lopsided, appearing to lean away from the direction of the beach. This is the windswept look that is so typical of plants, trees especially, growing near to the sea.

Fortunately there are many plants that are highly or moderately tolerant of salt. Amongst the former are *Agave*, *Hedera* (ivy), *Euonymus fortunei*, some junipers, *Liriope muscari* (lilyturf), *Magnolia grandiflora*, *Nerium oleander*, *Parthenocissus quinquefolia* (Virginia creeper), tamarisks, thymes and *Viburnum tinus* (laurustinus).

Plants that are moderately tolerant of salt, but which are best when planted in sheltered gardens or behind windbreaks, include *Agapanthus* (African lily), *Ageratum houstonianum* (flossflower), *Begonia semperflorens* (bedding begonia), *Calendula officianilis* (pot marigold), *Canna* (Indian shot plant), *Helianthus annuus* (sunflower), *Hemerocallis* (daylily), *Ligustrum* (privet), *Mahonia aquifolium* (Oregon grape), *Rosmarinus* (rosemary) and *Salvia officinalis* (sage).

There are a few garden plants that are tolerant of seawater flooding, but they will usually only remain unscathed if flooding occurs during the dormant part of the year. These plants include *Cytisus scoparius* (Scotch broom), *Elaeagnus*, *Salix* (willow) and *Sedum* 'Autumn Joy'.

RIGHT *Variegated century plant* (Agave americana 'Variegata').

EFFECTS OF SALT ON STRUCTURES

In the garden there are several structures on to which it is not desirable to have a salt layer. Iron and steel, found in wrought-iron garden gates and patio furniture, are the most obvious examples. When in contact with water and oxygen, or other strong oxidants or acids, iron will rust; if salt is present, as in sea water, the metal rusts much more quickly.

Galvanization is an important approach to rust prevention and this typically consists of a layer of zinc applied to the surface of the object to be protected (by either hot-dip galvanizing or electroplating). Zinc is traditionally used because it is cheap and adheres well to the steel. In situations where salt water is present, however, cadmium is preferred. Galvanization often fails at joints, seams and holes, where the coating is pierced, so applying proprietary rust preventatives may be useful at these points.

Valuable metal objects such as cars and boats should not be left to the full force of the salty elements without being protected or covered. And steel fixtures such as metal roofs and gazebos should be regularly treated with rust preventatives.

In the case of wooden furniture, regular exposure to salt water, or salty winds, will cause the wood to dry out more rapidly than it would do otherwise. Without treatment it will crack and split, which will allow access to burrowing insects and harmful microorganisms. Oak (*Quercus* spp) and teak (*Tectona* spp) are dense, close-grained hardwoods high in natural oils. These characteristics give them strength and durability, but they still benefit from protective oils, applied with oily rags at the end of autumn and the beginning of spring.

ABOVE *A contemporary house by the sea at Studland, in Dorset, UK, built using resilient modern materials.*

BELOW *Three examples of how long-term exposure to wind and salt air can affect structures and metals.*

Coastal conditions

SEA MIST AND FOG

Most of us have seen rolling swirls of mist or fog coming off the sea, heading inland. Technically, this is known as an 'advection' fog, and it is formed when warm air cools over a cold sea. Because sea surface temperature does not alter much in the short term, the fog usually persists over the sea until there is a change in wind direction. It may be patchy as well.

Sea fog can exist in wind speeds of up to 15mph (24km/h) because turbulence merely brings more warm air into contact with the cooling surface. If the wind is any stronger than this, it will lift the fog off the surface to give very low cloud. Fortunately, any fog which drifts across warming land, particularly during summer, usually disperses a short distance inland.

Interestingly, in warmer places this sea fog can exist in even greater strengths. For example, on a sunny morning in Los Angeles, when the Mojave Desert further inland heats up and causes a sea breeze to blow, sea fog from above the cold Pacific to the west of California can be brought onshore like a tide. But it disperses relatively quickly, as it spreads over the warming landmass.

Coastal dwellers should be prepared for a greater-than-average presence of mist and fog than is experienced by those living further inland, and of course there will be a proportion of salt water – although not great – present within the sea fog. This is not usually of sufficient strength to cause any greater damage to plants than the normal salt content of coastal air.

ABOVE *Sea mists can frequently be seen with a definite starting point and edge.*

LEFT *This mist appears to be rolling over the coastal hills in Devon, UK.*

BELOW *Sometimes the sea mist is more of a fog and, with no wind, can linger along the coastline for the whole day.*

BLOWN SAND

This is a greater problem than you might imagine. For example, a catastrophic sandstorm occurred at Culbin in Scotland at the end of the seventeenth century. There had been a richly diverse estate and farmstead there for centuries, but by the 1690s the sandbanks and dunes along the shores of the Moray Firth had been exposed, as a result of local people stripping the grasses for use as roofing thatch. In the autumn of 1694, a deep depression caused a yellow blizzard of sand which lasted all night and drifted high against the houses. After a short lull, the storm renewed and the whole village was then submerged in sand, forming an arid desert covering an area some 8 square miles (21km^2).

Occasional storms over the intervening years have reshaped the sand – sometimes exposing the tops of the still-buried houses. Since the 1920s the UK Forestry Commission has created plantations of grass, brushwood and young trees as a successful three-line defence against further wind and sandstorm damage.

In any coastal garden there will be a degree of blown sand. If the garden is particularly exposed or vulnerable to this, it would make sense to grow plants that are sturdy and able to withstand the onslaught. Many grasses are suitable, as the fine sand particles blow between the stems and blades, rather than against them.

Of course, even inland gardens can be covered in sand. In Europe sand falls from the sky occasionally, usually after being carried from the Sahara on high-altitude winds. But this is never in such a quantity as to damage plantings.

ABOVE *A sandstorm can whip up quickly if the right conditions prevail.*

LEFT *Sand blowing against grass plants on the beach gives them a curious tufted appearance.*

HEAT AND LIGHT

In coastal gardens the air is frequently clearer than inland, meaning greater light intensity and periods of intense heat in summer. High temperatures can induce several different problems with plants. One such is that of sun scald, which can arise when hot sun strikes the bark of thin-barked trees, such as beech (*Fagus* spp), cherries (*Prunus* spp), maples (*Acer* spp) and poplars (*Populus* spp). It can cause the death of the area of bark affected and, in severe cases, the whole tree.

The fruits of many plants that are grown for their produce may be similarly affected, such as tomatoes, apples, pears, gooseberries and grapes. If your garden is situated in an area known for its 'good' lighting in summer – such as the English town of St Ives (see page 15), which has been inhabited for centuries by artists who go there for its brilliant light and air quality – it may be safer to avoid using the plants mentioned above.

LEFT *Structures as well as plants can be drowned by shifting sands.*

SUBTROPICAL AND EXPOSED GARDENS

In the cool climes of Scandinavia and northern Europe, and on the prolific Canadian coastlines, you are fairly unlikely to come across exotic plantings with palms, bananas, cycads and bromeliads. These are all the sorts of plants at home in tropical rainforests – a far cry from the cooler countries.

Yet there are pockets of pleasure to be found. Take, for example, the Scilly Isles, situated 28 miles (45km) off the southwestern tip of Cornwall, England. These small islands, of which four are large enough to be inhabited, are set in the middle – seemingly – of the Atlantic Ocean, with no mainland in view. You would expect conditions here to be harsh and uncompromising, yet because the islands are situated in the currents of the Atlantic's Gulf Stream, both the sea and air temperatures are far warmer than one would usually expect for this latitude.

As a consequence, an amazing range of exotic-looking plants are able to be grown. One of the islands, Tresco, boasts a world-famous subtropical garden containing more than 20,000 plants, most of which are non-indigenous, but which nevertheless thrive – with no protection from wind and salt.

RIGHT *The island of Tresco as visitors first see it as they fly in by helicopter. In the centre of the picture is the Abbey building.*

BELOW Aeonium arboreum *in flower on Tresco.*

Tresco Abbey Gardens, Scilly Isles

Tresco, the second-largest island in the Scilly Isles group, features an amazing variety of scenery: wild rugged granite outcrops and heathland to the north, with subtropical sandy beaches and the Abbey Gardens in the south. This is because the unique microclimate at the sheltered southern tip of Tresco has formed a unique environment, with many species of plants thriving here that would not survive on the UK mainland.

The Abbey Gardens are home to more than 20,000 exotic plants from 80 countries across the globe (including Brazil, New Zealand and Africa).

The gardens were originally the private estate of Augustus Smith. He began to create this beautiful setting from the bare moorland around the old Priory following his appointment as Lord Proprietor of the Scillies in 1834. He constructed a series of walled enclosures and terraces on the rocky southern slopes of the island. Tall windbreaks channelled the weather up and over the site, sheltering the gardens from the worst of the weather.

By planting the hotter, drier terraces at the top with species imported from Australia and South Africa, and those at the bottom with species that prefer a more humid regime – such as plants from South America and New Zealand – he created a garden with a greater biodiversity than can be found anywhere in the Southern Mediterranean.

ABOVE *Some of the planting schemes in Tresco Abbey Gardens are breathtakingly beautiful, with alpine and rockery plants next to huge succulents, such as this* Agave.

PLAN: EXPOSED COASTAL GARDEN

Tresco Abbey Gardens has both formal and informal elements, and so does the garden in the plan shown here. If one followed this plan, and the planting choice was largely made up of exotic plants and succulents (and there are views of the sea, distant or otherwise), then the similarity to Tresco would be complete.

A   Terrace
B   Steps
C   Patio
D   Formal pond
E   Lawn
F   Path
G   Arch
H   Shrubbery
I   Woodland glade/seat
J   Wildlife pond
K   Garden office
L   Sculptures
M   Herbaceous border

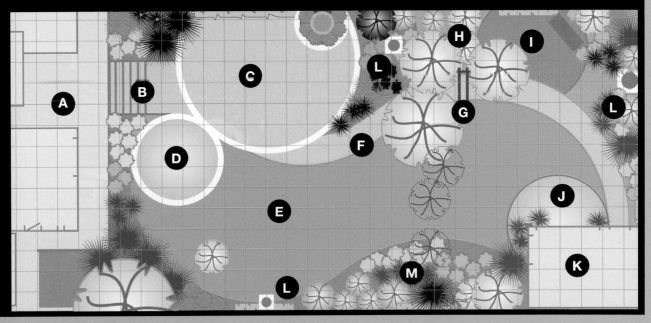

Plants at Tresco

Fringing the lush grid of paths criss crossing the subtropical space at Tresco Abbey Gardens are cacti, date palms and giant lipstick-red flame trees, with rarities such as lobster claw (Clianthus puniceus), great white spires of Echia, brilliant Furcraea, and bird of paradise (Strelitzia reginae), to shocking-pink drifts of Pelargonium.

Fittingly, the layout begins with the original plantings around the Priory and ends with the new, terraced Mediterranean Garden, a horticultural world tour condensed into 17 acres (6.8ha).

If led blindfold into the garden you would be hard-pressed to tell which region of the world you were in. The top terrace, with its sea views and open, sunny aspect, is home to many plants from the dry regions of Australia and South Africa; summer breezes and salty winter gales alike push through the foliage of Protea, Leucadendron, Aloe, Banksia, bottle brushes (Callistemon), Dryandra and Cape heaths (Erica hyemalis).

Moving lower down to the more protected slopes of the middle terrace, we move into a quite different plant grouping. Date palms (Phoenix dactylifera), Echium and Aeonium jostle for position with passionflowers (Passiflora spp), century plants (Agave spp) and Puya (which in its natural Chilean habitat would be pollinated by colourful hummingbirds).

Shadier parts of the garden at the base of the hillside reveal statuesque tree ferns (Dicksonia spp) from Australasia. Alongside grow towering gums (Eucalyptus spp) and the Norfolk Island pine (Araucaria excelsa).

The seasons at Tresco

At any time of the year the flowering capacity of the garden is amazing. The summer months reveal a mixture of colour from Mesembryanthemum, Pelargonium and Watsonia suffused with individual highlights such as Furcraea, Metrosideros and Abutilon.

The word 'winter' does not really exist on Tresco; the locals prefer to call it an extended autumn with flowering periods. Throughout November, December and January, the proteas, aloes and tree heaths are at their exotic best, with flowering camellias thrown in for good measure.

Statues and figurines, symbolizing the 'natural forces', accentuate the garden's overall beauty, whilst shipwrecked figureheads at the front of the Valhalla Museum remind you of the remoteness of these small islands.

Many people also believe that Tresco was the legendary 'Lyonesse', or 'land across the sea' – the final resting place of King Arthur.

LEFT *Decorative planting at Tresco with yellow* Dianthus, *mauve pelargoniums and the daisy flowers of* Erigeron.

LEFT The Succulent Rockery above the Old Abbey at Tresco.

RIGHT The Mediterranean Garden at Tresco.

RIGHT Views of the coastal waters, seen through some of Tresco's naturally growing palm trees.

Access to Tresco

Tresco Abbey Garden is open every day of the year to visitors. Access to the island is the main limiting factor.

By helicopter: from the Heliport at Penzance, Cornwall, the Sikorsky craft of British International Helicopters soars across Mounts Bay with its castle on St Michael's Mount, and swings southwest along the breathtaking coastline. The journey is just 20 minutes.

By sea: travel by sea aboard the Scillonian, which departs from Penzance, on the Cornish coast. The journey to Tresco takes 2hrs 40min.

By light aircraft: the final option is to fly via the Skybus from the English airports at Newquay, Exeter, Bristol and Southampton, as well as Land's End (the closest mainland airfield to the Scilly Isles, at the tip of Cornwall). Flights take you to the airfield on St Mary's, a neighbouring island, and you then need to hop on a quick ferry over to Tresco.

Chapter 3

THE VALUE OF GOOD GARDEN DESIGN

To look its best, a garden will usually need to be designed. It's perfectly acceptable, of course, for a garden to evolve, but the end result will probably be a hotchpotch of styles, with little in the way of cohesion. This is even more true of gardens that have natural restrictions, such as being near the coast.

RIGHT *It is a good idea to keep lovely sea views uncluttered by pots or furniture, as shown here at the Thompson Brookes Garden, San Francisco Bay, USA.*

Design basics

A GARDEN SITUATED close to the sea is almost certainly one of the most demanding in terms of design because shelter, wind protection, exposure to salt and, of course, the planting options all need special consideration.

Before you start designing your garden, you need to look at the things you cannot alter. For example, if you have a garden on a slope, you will need steps or sloping paths; once these are in place, the rest of the garden can be designed around them. Similarly, a garden predominately in the sun will need to have some shade introduced (for the owner to enjoy some respite during the hotter months). Conversely, a heavily shaded garden will need to have a lawn, patio or deck put down in a spot where the sun does fall, and there will be certain plants to choose or avoid.

FORMALITY V. INFORMALITY

In the context of garden design, 'formal' means the integration within the garden space of borders with straight edges, ponds in regular geometric shapes (circles, squares, rectangles and so on) and, of course, the use of clipped evergreens such as box (*Buxus* spp) and yew (*Taxus* spp). Flower beds in summer are quite likely to have straight rows of plants (in the style so beloved of parks the world over), and the mixed herbaceous borders will be traditional, with taller plants at the back, shorter at the front, blocks of colour and a straight edge.

People often assume that formal gardens are very labour-intensive; this is likely to be true if you have lots of sizeable evergreen hedges that need to be trimmed at least twice a year to keep them looking neat; otherwise a formal garden need not be any more time-consuming to look after than an informal space.

A lawn will generally have straight, well-kept edges, and the garden owner is likely to take pride in its appearance; a cylinder mower may well be used to cut it, resulting in that familiar stripe effect caused by the different directions in which the mower's roller has travelled. Informal gardens tend to have bed and lawn edges which are curved rather than straight.

ABOVE *This solid wall at the Eden Project, in Cornwall, UK, incorporates a long 'peephole' to view the garden beyond.*

BELOW *The planting should always be complementary to the surrounding architecture.*

Paths may be winding and look quite natural. Plants will be grouped by shape and height, rather than in straight rows. And there are usually many more colours, with pastels mixed with stronger primary shades. Plants are often used to break up the hard lines of path and bed edges too.

Part of an informal garden may also be a wild, or 'natural', garden, a style of gardening that is currently very popular. The idea is to establish a community of plants that will coexist happily, look natural, encourage insects, birds and wildlife, and quite possibly consist of native species.

ABOVE *Long, straight borders give a feeling of spaciousness and depth.*

ABOVE *Garden hideaways such as this tree house add a focal point, as well as a quiet place to relax.*

RIGHT *Water in the garden, whether a small pond or larger feature, can give an entirely different feel and an extra dimension.*

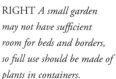

LEFT *A rustic bridge is the main access point to this small coastal garden.*

RIGHT *A small garden may not have sufficient room for beds and borders, so full use should be made of plants in containers.*

LEFT *Brick or block paving can make a small area look more spacious.*

BELOW LEFT *A typical coastal property, almost certainly with fine views of the sea.*

SIZE AND SHAPE

The size and shape of a garden, over which the gardener generally has no control, will dictate what you put in it and how you create your ideal space.

With regard to size, these days gardens are generally much smaller. As town and cities spread, land becomes more valuable, and developers are constantly striving to put more dwellings on given patches of land, which means that gardens – if they are provided at all – are diminishing.

But what is a 'small' garden? It's not easy to say, but it is quite likely that perception of size is directly related to the experience of the gardener. For example, beginners may find that a plot measuring some 20 by 30ft (6 by 9m) is quite large enough for them to cope with. More experienced gardeners, on the other hand, may not be satisfied unless they have something 10 times the size.

One of the secrets of success in designing a small garden is to make the best possible use of the space. The garden's different elements do not want to look crammed in and crowded, and the old adage of 'less is more' is usually true. Large gardens usually have the luxury of sizeable lawns, some big specimen trees and plants, water features and patios, and as a result are often easier to design.

Having a small garden invariably means that neighbouring gardens – and houses – are close by, which means that access points, pathways and boundaries take on a greater significance than in a large garden where a large tree or two, or a shrub border, can act as a screen.

The shape of the garden is also something over which the gardener usually has no control. A garden may be long and narrow, or short and wide. It may have two sides and a front and back, or it may have many 'ins' and 'outs', giving the opportunity for lots of interesting nooks and crannies. Or it may be a triangular shape, usually when it is at the end of a road where sides of the garden join others at obtuse angles. Or the garden may be mostly at the side of the property, with little in front of or behind it.

ASPECT

The 'aspect' is simply the direction in which your garden faces. One of the first questions a keen gardener should ask when looking for a new house to buy or rent is: 'Which way does the garden face?'

Ideally you should go for a garden that faces the sun. In fact, even if you are not a gardener, but you do enjoy sitting out and relaxing in the sun, you will want a garden that faces towards it.

The direction towards the sun will vary according to where you live in the world: in the northern hemisphere the garden should face southwards, and in the southern hemisphere it should face northwards. If your plot faces east or west, wherever you are on the planet, you will have early morning or late afternoon sun respectively.

Having a sunny garden means that, particularly in the summer months, the major part of the garden will bask in the glory of full sun. During the longest days, when the sun is at its highest in the sky, your garden could – if you are not careful – become a desert. If you plant the wrong types of plant in a sunny position, or if you fail to give the plants the correct amount of moisture to allow them to thrive, at worst you could be consigning them to an early death and at best they will become very poor specimens. And, of course, it would mean that your garden will be baked and barren.

This is a common occurrence near the coast, for many properties are used only sporadically throughout the year, meaning that there is not always someone around to irrigate, prune or otherwise tend the plants when they most need it.

RIGHT *The sunniest aspect, especially in warmer regions, will be perfect for growing cacti and succulents.*

ABOVE *Rustic steps leading to a sheltered sitting area.*

LEFT *Thrift* (Armeria maritima) *growing high on a coastal clifftop.*

TOPOGRAPHY

Although topography is the posh word for the study of the Earth's surface, including vegetative and human-made features, in terms of garden design, topography specifically involves the way the ground falls. Does the garden undulate – that is, have bumps and hollows – or is there a definite slope and, if so, how steep? A very large garden can, of course, include all of these things, which makes the design more challenging, but hugely rewarding.

Few gardens are exactly level, even if they appear to be so. The smallest changes of level can be used to advantage with the installation of a few wide steps and/or one or two low retaining walls. These could make a flattish site look much more interesting. You may also decide to create a steeper gradient to make a feature; this will inevitably mean moving a large amount of soil and either strenuous effort or added expense if you bring in the labour.

A steeply sloping garden, either natural or man-made, can suffer from several problems, including poor access, lack of useable level areas, soil erosion and either permanently damp spots at the bottom of the slope or permanently dry spots at the top (or both). Again, steps can be used to reduce

or eliminate the problems of a steep garden. If for reasons of cost or practicality steps are not possible, you could consider a careful selection of planting, with perhaps heavy mulching between the plants, to make the garden attractive and low-maintenance.

A gently sloping garden is much easier to cope with; winding paths or ramps can be used to allow access for people with limited mobility or where garden machinery and wheelbarrows need to traverse. They offer much in terms of design potential as well, with raised patios and terraces, and opportunities for water gardens where you may be able to look down on them, and so on.

Terraces

The word 'terrace' is used to describe a flat area in an otherwise sloping garden. Such areas may be linked by steps or ramps, and can be created by the construction of retaining walls. Of course, as the slope increases, the height of any necessary retaining wall increases accordingly, and you may need expert help to construct it.

RIGHT *This garden is on a steep slope, and the pond forms its own terrace.*

Rock gardens and water gardens

A garden with a slope provides good opportunities for features such as a rock garden or a water garden, or a combination of the two. In the case of the former, you should use locally occurring stone for the rocks, and they should be set so as to look as natural as possible. The best-looking rock gardens are designed as an integral part of the complete garden, rather than being a random feature, sited on their own in the middle of a lawn or paved area, as is often seen. A rock garden can be built in association with water features – ponds, waterfalls, cascades and streams – and an existing slope is ideal for this.

Scree gardens

A scree garden is one step away from a beach-like feature and is arguably entirely at home in a coastal garden. Screes are found naturally on the lower slopes of mountainous and alpine regions, where small fragments of rock fall from the upper slopes. They accumulate and over time create a special set of growing conditions where tight, bushy plants, often with a cushion-like appearance, are most at home. Scree gardens look particularly effective at the lower edge of a larger rock garden.

ABOVE *A border with architectural quality – blue sea holly, yellow yarrow and seedheads of the African lily.*

BELOW *The path to the front door rises with a series of steps.*

LEFT AND BELOW *Gravel gardens with natural plantings.*

DESIRABILITY OF VIEWS

Without doubt the best coastal gardens, whether large or small, are those that afford a beautiful view. The view maybe out to sea or across a bay, or it could be facing inland, with a scene of rolling fields and far-off hills laid out before you.

Properties with wonderful views always command premium prices, but it is surprising how often you see garden owners failing to capitalize on these views. Views can easily be obscured by overgrowing trees and vegetation, or perhaps you have to scramble to a remote or difficult part of the garden in order to take in the view.

In the case of the former, cut back overhanging branches or lop the tops of trees as necessary. However, this should be done carefully. Some trees have orders placed on them that makes it illegal to remove or substantially alter them without prior approval by the local authority.

A view that can be seen only from a remote or difficult-to-access part of the garden will require a little more planning. Perhaps the access could be improved: this may require the widening – or creating – of paths, and it may also necessitate the repositioning of beds and borders, or even moving around existing plants.

Regardless of any of this, it should be the aim of the garden owner always to install a seating or patio area at the place where the view is best.

BELOW Balcony overlooking a swimming pool and the sea.

ABOVE Open coastal views in Taupo Bay, New Zealand.

BELOW Swimming pool and ocean view (left) and views of a bay in Turkey through an old olive grove (right).

FRONT GARDENS

It is rare to find a property with a front and rear garden where both seamlessly merge so that they form a continuous 'flow' – with the house situated somewhere in the middle. In most cases a front garden will appear quite different from the rear, and is used for different purposes. It may, for example,

be kept tidy, as people will see it as they walk by, but because it is on view it can also mean that the gardener does not consider it to be a 'private' area, unlike the rear garden which is generally hidden from the public gaze.

A front garden will also need to allow for good access and possibly the movement of vehicles. In both cases a successful layout comes down to making sure there is space for:

- People to assemble by the front door
- People to get in and out of a car
- Parking and possibly turning for cars.

A garden can then be created, hopefully, in the space that is left after these considerations have been made.

LEFT AND ABOVE
Three examples of seaside front gardens in New Zealand, with a wide range of native plants.

WALKWAYS

In the front garden, walkways should be simple, straightforward affairs, designed purely to take people from the boundary entrance to the house in the most expedient way. A straight line, therefore, is usually chosen. In some cases the driveway for the car may also suffice as the walkway, but in these cases you should make sure that the driveway has sufficient width to accommodate both a car and people walking alongside it.

In the back garden paths and walkways offer a very different proposition. Here they can wind and meander their way down or across the plot. They should always be:

- Wide enough to allow access for things such as wheelbarrows and lawn mowers
- Kept clear of dangerously spiky or thorny plants
- Have a sound and even base to avoid accidents.

If your garden is close enough to the sea to afford a good view, then a pathway leading to a viewpoint, with a strategically placed bench seat, can become a favourite place.

Garden structures

AN IMPORTANT FACTOR in the design of any garden, coastal or otherwise, is being able to identify those spots where the microclimate is suitable – or unsuitable – for particular needs. You can then plan how and where you put your garden structures such as patios, shelters and archways that make the most of these areas.

PATIOS AND DECKING

A patio is traditionally located near the back door of the house. But if the back of the house faces away from the sun, the chances are the patio is best situated farther down the garden, where the sun's rays will fall to the ground without being shaded by the house itself. Clearly, this is where the owner of a large garden has an advantage over those with smaller spaces.

If you do need to site a patio some distance from the house, you will need to pave an area leading from one to the other, and this will mean that more landscaping materials will be required and the overall cost will rise. Such patios also frequently benefit from a planted backdrop, so that people can relax and feel at least partly secluded. Patios built out in the open, with no surrounding plants or structures, rarely feel comfortable.

Wooden decking seems appropriate to a coastal garden – it's probably something to do with wooden beach walkways, wooden jetties and piers, and boat decking. Wood is certainly a durable, attractive and appropriate material in a coastal garden setting, but you should watch out for rotting in salty and exposed situations. Mildew and other deposits which may collect on the deck are best cleaned by scrubbing or low-pressure spraying. Using chemical cleaners is not recommended, as these may harm the wood; like salt, they could raise the grain or alter the colour of the deck – or both.

SITING FIXTURES

There are several features in gardens that might be regarded as 'fixtures and fittings', that is, things that can't easily be moved. It is important to choose the right place for them at the outset, to avoid any mess and upheaval in resiting them.

Mostly these are the features that need to be in the sun, such as sitting areas, greenhouses, conservatories, fruit and vegetable plots, most flower beds and borders, rockeries and swimming pools. Ponds and water features do not need as much direct sunlight (although some is desirable), but neither these nor swimming pools want to be near to trees, as the falling leaves can wreak havoc in the water.

If a barbecue area is to be installed, some evening sunshine is desirable; if a greenhouse is to be erected, choose a place that gets good light in the early part of the year so that seedlings can soak up the sun's rays unhindered.

Shaded areas, such as those caused by walls or fences, are not ideal for growing vegetables, although there are some types that don't mind a little shade during the day. A very shaded garden will still produce reasonable crops of Jerusalem artichokes, corn salad, rocket, spinach, watercress and even rhubarb.

Areas of least sunlight can be used for siting sheds, compost heaps, general storage areas and the driveway for the car.

ABOVE *A small deck looks better with one sizeable item of furniture rather than many smaller items.*

RIGHT *A simple pool area enhanced with neatly arranged containers.*

BELOW *Modern and traditional greenhouses – functional fixtures that, if well designed, can also be pleasing to look at.*

DESIRABILITY OF HEIGHT

With small gardens very often the only way to go is up! An archway, which can accommodate a climbing plant or two may be desirable therefore, but it may be too small to be effective. Better still, a timber pergola – which is essentially a series of two or more attached arches – could be built if there is available space.

Pergolas are most often found on a patio and/or close to the house. This is so that you can sit under them, and perhaps be sheltered from the heat of the summer sun. But a freestanding pergola can be placed anywhere in the garden. If it is away from the patio, there needs to be a 'reason' for it in design terms, and this reason could be, for example, to walk through it to see a little statue situated at the far end, or it could be a walkway through to a vegetable- or fruit-growing area.

On a patio a pergola could be set next to small raised beds where coastal plants can be grown. Alternatively, if your pergola is over a garden path, you can grow plants in narrow borders on each side of the path.

'Arbour' is the name for a sitting area and is so called because it was originally surrounded by trees. Today it usually means a sitting area with a canopy of wood above you, often designed simply to act as a shade from the sun.

Regardless of where and why you erect an arch, pergola or arbour, all are entirely appropriate in a coastal garden, provided the plants growing on them are tolerant of salty winds.

Windy gardens, as we have already seen, can be made more comfortable, for plants and humans alike, through the filtering effects of trees and windbreaks. These also add height, of course, and there are two rules to which any garden designer should adhere: namely balance and proportion. Both will have to be applied to trees and windbreaks so that they end up looking appropriate. For example, take a grouping of three new trees. If they are to be viewed from one side only, it would be sensible to start off with them at different heights, with the tallest one farthest from view.

LEFT *A typical French courtyard is enhanced by a selection of taller plants and trees.*

ABOVE *Rustic arch with a vigorous kiwi fruit vine.*

LEFT *A well-covered pergola provides a shaded seating area.*

BELOW *Orchid-covered, arched walkways in a garden surrounded by rainforest, in Singapore, Southeast Asia.*

SHELTER MATERIALS

Finally, in terms of garden design, we must come back to the most important element that affects how we garden in a coastal situation – exposure to wind. In Chapter 2 we looked at the main ways in which wind speed can be reduced. We know therefore how windbreaks, walls, fences and hedges help in this regard.

In design terms, however, there is also the material element. If, for example, you want to put up a wall to provide shelter for yourself and/or your plants, should it be made from expensive brick, cheaper rendered block walling, decorative open-cast screen-block walling, or rustic mortared stone and dry-stone?

Each type will produce the same benefits, but will look completely different and determine the design of the garden in the immediate vicinity. Similarly, the choice of fencing or natural screen can influence the style of garden around it.

Part Two

COASTAL *garden style*

Stylish living is what many of us strive for, and this usually manifests itself in the way we decorate and furnish our homes. But our gardens can also be incredibly stylish, and how we create and maintain them can say a great deal about us as individuals.

Chapter 4

SHORELINE GARDENS

 It takes a brave person to start a garden just a few metres from the sea's edge. We have already learned that the wind, sand and strong saline conditions can cause havoc in such situations. If these are overcome, however, the rewards (and the views) can be well worth the effort.

RIGHT *Those who garden on the shoreline can learn much from the plants that grow naturally in the vicinity.*

Gardening by the sea

WIND STRAIGHT OFF the sea damages plants in several ways. Of course there is the obvious matter of branches falling from trees and, in severe instances, the trees themselves toppling over. But in the long term, wind and salt cause plants to be stunted, with smaller foliage and shortened branches. Tender shoots and buds emerging in spring are frequently 'burnt' by wind and salt, but extreme sunlight can also take its toll on these.

The strategy to deal with these conditions is to:
• Put up planted windbreaks or artificial screens/fences
• Choose plants that are tough and suited to such conditions.

If the garden is situated to the rear of a sandy beach, then there is another element that must be considered: planting in sand.

SOILS OF SAND

Those who have to plant in sandy soil undeniably face greater gardening obstacles than almost anyone else. The main problem with a soil that is mostly sand is that it drains instantly and retains very little moisture, so plants growing in it must be highly drought-tolerant.

A secondary problem with sand is that it gets hot; the relentless summer sun can make it burning to the touch, so plants growing in it must also tolerate extreme heat. Foggy or rainy days at the beach may be loathed by holiday-makers, but they are essential for these plants – even if these cooler conditions give only short-term respite.

In conventional gardening the rule is always that, before plants are planted, the soil should be prepared – dug, weeded and, if the soil is 'hungry', well-rotted compost or manure should be incorporated into it. In thin, sandy, fast-draining soils, organic matter like this helps to retain

ABOVE *Coastal properties built on the edge of sandy beaches pose immense challenges to the gardener. Drought-tolerant plants such as* Lampranthus spectabilis *thrive in these types of conditions.*

RIGHT *Drought is a real problem on sandy soils.*

essential moisture. Luckily, those living near to the sea have a ready source of organic matter – seaweed (see page 94).

Interestingly, planting in the dry sandy dunes set back from the water's edge is more difficult than right at the shoreline because the groundwater level at the dunes is much deeper and therefore less accessible to plant roots.

At the water's edge the groundwater is somewhat higher and the air is damp with spray. However, planting here is suitable only for those plants that are extremely tolerant of salt-laden spray and groundwater.

THE IMPORTANCE OF FRESH WATER

Trees and shrubs are, without doubt, the thirstiest of a seashore garden's network of permanent plants. Just think about how much water a mature 60ft (18m) tree needs to absorb to fill all of its growing cells – every day. The good news is that a tree of this size will usually be able to look after itself; its roots will penetrate far and deep, and will tap in to the water table.

The most crucial period for a tree to be given supplementary water is during the first few years after planting. Watering – with fresh water, never sea water – at planting time settles the sand or soil particles around the roots, enabling newly developed root hairs to take up water.

But new roots will take time to develop and search out water, so adequate supply needs to be on hand as the leaf canopy develops and the tree demands increasingly more water.

Smaller perennial and bedding plants will usually appreciate quite a bit of supplementary watering during hot weather – the bedding plants usually showing signs of dehydration before the perennials. If the area is densely planted, a sprinkler may be employed to good effect, but make sure that the water spray does not land on uncultivated ground for this would be a serious waste of water.

Bulbous plants tend to have their own reserves of moisture stored within the bulb. The few fleshy roots that emit from the base of the bulbs are there to absorb supplementary soil moisture when the bulbs start to get dry.

ABOVE *A garden that gently merges with the native flora keeps watering to a minimum.*

BELOW *Watering from a hosepipe uses lots of water, but you can direct it to where it is needed.*

BELOW RIGHT *Trickle irrigation can be laid out in between plants to ensure that they get enough water.*

RULES OF PLANTING

Part of the success in establishing plants in these hostile conditions is in planting them whilst they are small. They are easier to plant when small, they are more likely to survive and, because they are cheaper, you can choose more of them.

If you are planting an area that is devoid of plants, and you have a 'blank canvas', it is a good idea to set out the plants whilst they are still in their pots. This will give you an idea of what the eventual display will look like (although you will need a little imagination to visualize them when fully grown). Most plant labels give dimensions of height and spread when the plants are fully grown, and it is important to take note of these.

You can then improve the spacings and placings accordingly. It is all too easy to set out plants too close to each other, which can encourage weak and spindly growth. Conversely, in aesthetic terms, gardeners often space the plants too far apart, and the border, or dune, can look sparse.

Just before you put any of these plants in the ground, apply a dressing of bonemeal fertilizer over the area at the rate of 2oz per sq yd (65g per m²). Work it into the surface of the sandy soil, using a hoe or rake, tread the area until firm, then rake it until it is level.

ABOVE *Position and space plants out before deciding on their final arrangement.*

RIGHT *Local flower fairs such as this one in southern France are ideal for getting more unusual plants straight from the growers.*

STAKING

In many sheltered gardens, it is not always absolutely necessary to stake trees (although gardening books always tell you to). However, because a garden on the shoreline is so exposed, a stake should always be used to support small trees. It should be driven into the hole before planting the tree, so as to avoid damaging the tree's roots. The top of the stake should come up just to the base of the first outward branches, to avoid unnecessary rubbing.

WHERE TO SOURCE PLANTS

Finding places that sell these hardcore maritime plants is not always easy, but we do list a few international suppliers at the back of this book. Even as recently as 1990, it was almost impossible to find specialists in salt-, wind- and sand-tolerant plants, and you are even today unlikely to find them for sale in traditional garden centres.

However, gardening tastes have changed considerably over the past few decades, and the current fashions for natural, wild and wildlife-friendly gardens have allowed more of our desirable seaside plants to become available. Also, as we will discover later in the book, many conventional garden plants, somewhat surprisingly, are able to cope admirably with the conditions found at the shoreline.

SUBTROPICAL AND SHELTERED GARDENS

When we looked at the island of Tresco (pages 40-43), we discovered how exotic-looking subtropical plants were able to be grown in the UK, even though they were fully exposed to wind and salt spray. This was thanks entirely to the warm currents of the Atlantic Gulf Stream. Islands, especially small ones out in the open ocean, have very little – or nothing – to prevent them from being blasted by gale-force winds on a regular basis. So the plants growing on Tresco, and the other Scillies, have to be tough against everything except the severe cold. They are certainly wind-tolerant and notably salt-tolerant.

But just think about the far greater diversity of plants available to you if your garden enjoys the warm Gulf waters, yet is also protected from those devastating winds. This is the Utopian environment enjoyed by the plants – and the gardeners – at Abbotsbury Subtropical Gardens in Dorset, on England's south coast.

RIGHT *Subtropical woodland planting at Abbotsbury.*

BELOW *Ornamental bench seating surrounded by exotic planting makes a lovely feature.*

Abbotsbury Subtropical Gardens, Dorset, UK

These gardens were established in 1765 by the first Countess of Ilchester, as a kitchen garden for her nearby castle. They have since developed into magnificent 20-acre (8ha) gardens filled with rare and exotic plants from all over the world. Many of these plants were first introductions to the UK, discovered by the plant-hunting descendants of the Countess. Abbotsbury has been claimed to have some of the best gardens of their type in the world.

The gardens are a mixture of formal and informal. There is a magnificent Victorian walled garden set in a woodland valley. And it is this valley that is the key to the success of the garden, for the stiff Atlantic gales, which whip straight off the adjoining Chesil Beach, sweep right over the top of the garden. The unique micro-climate, comprising warm maritime air with a low wind count, means that rare and exotic plant species from all over the world thrive here. Sunken gardens, a colonial style teahouse with veranda and scenic views of the golden World Heritage Coast, complete the scene at Abbotsbury (see page 188 for details).

ABOVE *A Greek-style urn makes a focal point in an open area at Abbotsbury. Banana plants are situated to the left and right.*

PLAN: A SHELTERED COASTAL GARDEN

The natural – and fortunate – phenomenon that protects Abbotsbury Subtropical Gardens from the elements is the high ridge between them and the beach. In a small garden, the protection is provided by surrounding walls and buildings. This plan is one way to capitalize on this protection. A contemporary circular sunken patio is accompanied by circular or arced pond, beds and steps. Combined strategic planting and uplighting will give the area the appearance of the subtropical.

A Sunken patio
B Pond wih uplighters
C Waterfall
D Sculpture
E Stone ridge
F Bench
G Access steps
H Uplighters
I Palms
J Scented planting
K Ground cover planting
L Palms
M Bamboos
N Seasonal colour

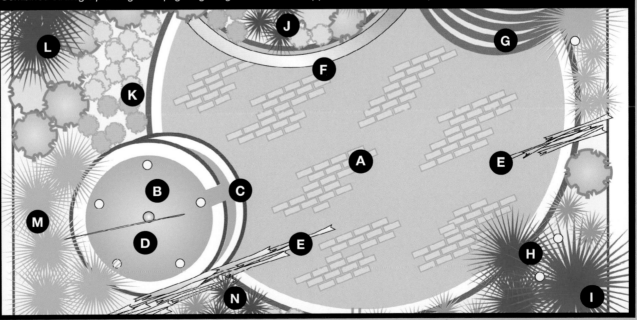

LEFT *White fence forming part of the entrance to Abbotsbury.*

RIGHT *The large, exotic foliage of* Ensete ventricosum *– a relative of the banana.*

Abbotsbury's plants

Walk through the valley garden and you will see tender woodland camellia groves and magnolias that you will not see anywhere else in the UK. Multicoloured Asiatic primroses border the banks of a stream in springtime, and there are many fine specimen trees and shrubs – particularly hydrangeas and rhododendrons. In the past decade many new exotic and unusual plants have been introduced.

Visitors can also take time to visit nearby Chesil Beach – which is 18 miles (30km) long and is said to contain 180 billion pebbles – with its display of wild coastal plants, especially good in June and July.

The Royal Botanic Gardens, Sydney

The Royal Botanic Gardens (RBG) in Sydney, Australia, provide an oasis of 74 acres (30ha) in the heart of the city (see page 188 for details).

Wrapped around Farm Cove at the edge of Sydney Harbour (the world's largest natural harbour), the gardens occupy a spectacular position. They are just a short walk around the water's edge from the Sydney Opera House and fill an area of land between the salt-water harbour and the eastern part of the central business district. The undulating piece of land on which the gardens sit offers both sheltered planting space in the dips and exposed planting space on the heights (from where the harbour views are superb).

Established in 1816, the Botanic Gardens Trust is the oldest scientific institution in Australia and home to an outstanding collection of plants. There are large trees with a wonderful shade canvas against the intense Australian summer sun, and there are a staggering one million cultivated plants to see.

Plants featured at RBG Sydney

Begonias: These magnificent plants are grown worldwide in the tropics and sub tropics for both flowers and foliage. A large garden devoted to them (sponsored by the Begonia Society of New South Wales) has been created at the gardens, where visitors can learn about the origins of these diverse plants – and how to grow them.

Herbs: Plants from around the world are on display in the gardens in a special herb garden. There is also a sensory fountain and sundial modelled on the celestial sphere.

Palms: A Palm Grove, established in 1862, is a cool summer haven and one of the world's finest collections of palms. Several of the Royal Botanic Gardens' oldest trees, grown from wild plants collected in the 1820s and 1850s, grow here.

Roses: The new Palace Rose Garden opened in 2006.

Succulents: Desert landscapes are a mosaic of colours, shapes and textures. The Succulent Garden provides a rare opportunity to experience and closely examine the bizarre shapes of arid-adapted plants.

The Wollemi Pine (pictured above): This ancient tree is one of the world's rarest plants, with only three stands of adult trees growing in the Blue Mountains of New South Wales. The first specimen ever planted out is growing here, in the sheltered, salty air of Sydney's Royal Botanic Gardens.

Chapter 5

SHELTERED GARDENS

In gardening, it is impossible to achieve the perfect plot. In an ideal world, a garden should be big, but not too big and certainly not too small. It should be level for ease of working, but have slopes and undulations to add interest. It should also be sheltered to ward off the worst of the elements, yet be open enough to give a feeling of space and to maximize views.

RIGHT *This garden strikes a fine balance. The plants provide shelter from the elements, but there are still gaps to allow the views to be enjoyed.*

Types of sheltered garden

ESSENTIALLY, a 'sheltered garden' is one where walls provide a kind of warm microclimate: they face the sun and are protected from cold winds. The garden should not be a haven for cold air either: it should 'drain away' without lingering.

The walls provide conditions that are ideal for tender plants, protecting them from the coldest weather and enhancing the warmest weather.

You can have a sheltered garden that is protected by tall trees and shrubs, but if the garden is also quite small it will probably be shady, and the ground could be congested with the roots of the windbreak plants. This is not a good combination. A large sheltered garden, on the other hand, sounds ideal, but is rarely found, for the bigger the plot, the greater the chances of exposure to wind.

For the purposes of this chapter, therefore, a sheltered garden is assumed to be medium to small, with a proportion of protective walls and screening plants that are not too invasive.

BELOW *Traditional Roman-style sheltered courtyard garden in Kalkan, southern Turkey.*

THE 'CORRIDOR' EFFECT

Gardens that are long and narrow present a challenge to the gardener. It can be difficult to know how to put everything you want into the area without it looking claustrophobic. Such gardens, especially if they have walls or fences running the length of each side, have been likened to horticultural 'corridors'.

The aim should always be to design long, narrow gardens to create a feeling of space. You can do this by developing the garden into separate areas, or 'rooms'. Each one should be different in character, yet they should all link together.

At the same time you should try to disguise the boundaries with plants or other features, such as ponds, rockeries, trelliswork at angles to the perimeter, and so on.

Where the soil is poor, containers can be used to great effect. These also allow you to grow chalk-loving plants if the soil is acidic, or acid-loving plants if the soil is chalky.

Containers also raise the heights and levels of plants slightly, so with careful and strategic placing of containers you can effectively bring another dimension to your garden.

ABOVE *In hot countries (this is the steamy Bay of Islands, New Zealand), a sheltered garden can also be used to provide useful shade.*

BELOW *Colourful* Osteospermum *growing on top of a coastal wall, sheltered by higher ground.*

ABOVE *Town garden utilizing strong structures with a large pond.*

COASTAL TOWN GARDENS

Mention 'town gardens' and you automatically think of small gardens in large towns and cities, most of which will be inland. However, there are thousands of towns worldwide that are within 15 miles (24km) of the sea, and so there are millions of town gardens that come within the subject of this book.

The smallest town gardens present a real challenge, especially to gardeners keen to grow as wide a range of plants as possible. Shelter from the walls of buildings and boundaries is a certainty, but there is also a likelihood of other problems, such as draughts, shade and poor, often rubble-filled soil. There are plants that accept such conditions, but will they also tolerate salty air? Fortunately there are a few, including the spotted laurel (*Aucuba japonica* 'Variegata'), silk tassel bush (*Garrya elliptica*) and various ivies (*Hedera* spp) and hollies (*Ilex* spp).

Of course, sheltered coastal town gardens also offer great potential as well. For example, the warmth offered by walls facing the sun can be considerable – real sun traps – and the fact that walls tend to deflect much of the rain that falls means that you may be able to keep hardy (and a few tender) succulents and even cacti. Such hot, sun-loving plants will, by necessity, be just a few metres from a shady wall where it will be more appropriate to grow cool-loving woodland plants, giving you an interesting range of plant choices.

Finally, in a town garden where high walls are commonplace, and indeed there may be more vertical than horizontal spaces, there is every opportunity to grow a rich variety of climbing plants, such as the brilliant red flame creeper (*Tropaeolum speciosum*) and the blue passion flower (*Passiflora caerulea*). These will do much to engender the feeling of a green island in an urban desert.

LEFT *A peaceful courtyard planted with hardy plants, including a vine,* Clematis, *box, lavender,* iris, *hollyhocks and castor oil plant* (Fatsia).

Choice of plants

A SHELTERED COASTAL GARDEN enables you to grow an entirely different range of plants to those in gardens with exposed or windy conditions. You still need to choose plants that are able to grow in an area where there is salt in the air, but the shelter from surrounding walls also protects plants from the intensity of salt air and deposit, so it may occasionally be possible to grow plants that are rather more intolerant of salt.

With a sheltered garden there is a wide diversity of species available. Exotic foliage plants, such as the cabbage palm (*Cordyline australis*), Adam's needle (*Yucca filamentosa*) and the false castor oil plant or Japanese fatsia (*Fatsia japonica*) are in their element and can form the basis of such a garden. Combine them with showy, free-flowering shrubs such as oleander (*Nerium oleander*), laurustinus (*Viburnum tinus*) and Scotch broom (*Cytisus scoparius*) to make a truly exciting planting.

PROTECTING TENDER PLANTS FROM COLD

Unfortunately many of the plants that are suited to sheltered gardens are also plants that dislike very cold conditions so there is always a possibility that such tender plants will be killed off in a cold winter.

This can be avoided to some extent if the roots and lower parts of the plants are protected by insulating materials. These could be in the form of layers of mulching material – well-rotted compost and manure (which will also nourish the soil), or straw. Large containers housing tender plants may be wrapped with bubble-plastic to help protect the roots from the intense cold.

Luckily, many of the plants in a sheltered border are quick growing and are thus well able to spring up again from the base. Some will also be easy to propagate, enabling you (if you have the inclination) to keep a few substitute plants, in pots perhaps, as a sort of insurance policy.

ABOVE LEFT Solanum crispum '*Glasnevin*'.

ABOVE Clematis '*Ruby Glow*' covers a fence.

RIGHT *Red* Bougainvillea *on weatherboard cladding.*

LEFT *Pale lilac* Wisteria.

BELOW *A French house completely covered with Virginia creeper.*

SUPPORTING AND TRAINING PLANTS

Plants growing against or in front of walls are not the same as those growing up them. The former are referred to as 'wall plants', whereas the latter are most definitely 'climbers' (for a list of recommended plants, see pages 164–71).

One of the best methods of training plants onto, say, a brick wall in a coastal situation is to fix stout galvanized wires horizontally to the wall or, in the case of twining climbers, vertically. Wires should be set from 8–12in (20–30cm) apart and held in position at regular intervals by hooked or eyelet-holed metal pins, known as 'vive eyes', driven into the wall. Strong hooks can also be used. Both the wires and the hooks or eyes should be galvanized so that they do not rust away in the salt-laden air.

Strips of plastic-coated steel or wire netting fixed to the walls are also effective. This is very strong, comes in different sizes and meshes, and is fairly resistant to rust, although in time the plastic coating can flake away.

Another method of support is the trelliswork mentioned above. This comes in panels comprising a latticework of narrow laths, coated with wood preservative or paint. The panels can be easily fixed to the wall and held firm with the aid of wall plugs, screws or nails.

TERRACES AND SPLIT LEVELS

It is only in the past 60 or 70 years that home owners have desired split-level designs inside their homes. The aim was not to save space, but to give an extra dimension to the living space and be creative with the interior décor. Originally the split levels were made out of necessity because the house was on a slope; more recently, though, they have been built into homes on the flat, as features.

Outside, however, split-level gardens have been tended for thousands of years. The topography of the land frequently makes it necessary to create terraces which, in this context, are used to denote flat areas on otherwise sloping ground. By interrupting an incline and creating a flat area, one is able to cultivate plants efficiently, enabling better irrigation and allowing best sunlight. Crops and decorative plants can be grown to perfection, where previously indigenous and ground cover plants would be all that would grow successfully.

Coastal gardens are often sited on dramatically undulating ground, and for this reason many are designed in a split-level fashion.

RIGHT *The Dell Garden at Bodnant.*

BELOW *Raised beds are a convenient way to 'disguise' changes in level in a garden.*

Bodnant, North Wales, UK

Bodnant is an 80-acre (32ha) garden set just a few miles inland from the coast of North Wales. It is not merely one of the prettiest places in the UK to visit, but it also has a collection of plants that make it globally important (see page 188 for details).

Visitors are captivated first by the house, then the views from the various terraces overlooking the lawns and across the valley to the Carneddau mountains and Snowdonia National Park. Usually, it is only then, after having absorbed all of this, that you notice the exquisite garden.

In the late nineteenth century, the then owner planted various shrubberies, formal beds and also the famous Laburnum Walk, which in late May and early June is an overwhelming mass of bloom.

There are so many aspects and facets, features and surprises, particularly in spring, that you really need to be there a week to see everything and to do it all justice.

ABOVE Bodnant Hall is the house that goes with the 80-acre (32ha) estate.

PLAN: SPLIT-LEVEL COASTAL GARDEN

This plan is the design for a sloping garden surrounding a block of apartments, but could just as easily be created for a single, private dwelling. The terrace (C) is the lowest point of the garden, with the surrounding beds rising up and away. To avoid a 'hemmed in' appearance, the planting is kept deliberately open and sparse, with low-growing grasses and architecturally interesting plants, such as palms and phormiums.

A   Apartments
B   Balconies
C   Lower level terrace
D   Sloping driveway
E   Utilities
F   Water feature
G   Pebbles and grasses
H   Pebbles and grasses
I   Phormiums
J   Cordylines
K   Pebbles and grasses
L   Large cordylines
M   Large cordylines
N   Palms
O   Screening shrubs
P   Retaining walls

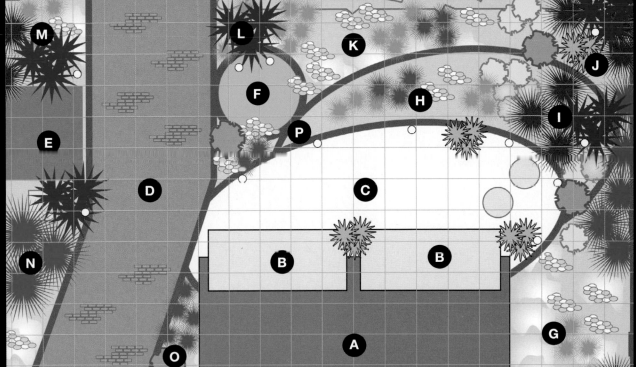

Terraces at Bodnant

Bodnant combines dramatic formal terraces with extensive woodland plantings on the grandest of scales. A deep herbaceous border, backing on to a high wall, is instantly striking, with mature, often tender climbers rampant above bold, warm plantings.

Beside the house, two enormous cedars overshadow a formal lily pond; they are set on the first of a succession of terraces, where hydrangeas abound. A crisply shaved yew hedge curves above a mezzanine rose pergola. On the Canal Terrace is a stately gazebo, the Pin Mill. It was originally constructed around 1730, some 100 miles (160km) away in the county of Gloucestershire, as a garden house attached to an Elizabethan residence. In 1938 the roof, timbers and the dressed stonework were brought to Bodnant, and encased in a new brick, stucco-covered building.

Near the house there is the rose terrace but, with some irony, roses almost take backstage position. And the lily terrace is named after the stretch of water that contains many summer-flowering waterlilies planted in underwater boxes; as many as 1,000 blooms have been open at one time.

Plants at Bodnant

Pencil-thin cypresses, with many cultivars of potentilla and cistus, help to create a Mediterranean feel on clear, sunny days. Along the stream there are meconopsis, hostas and bergenias.

There are a number of rose beds on the rose terrace, but they are edged with saxifrages, helianthemums and dwarf campanulas. There is a prominent and vast strawberry tree (Arbutus x andrachnoides), with gracefully curved red stems and upright foliage. Beyond this are various climbers, with rhododendrons, pieris and camellias.

In the dell garden is the tallest redwood in Wales, the 147ft (45m) Sequoia sempervirens. Some of the massive sequoiadendron trees bear planting plaques, which show them to be well in to their second century.

Other feature plants include escallonias, syringes (lilacs), white wisterias, acers, sorbus and red-flowered embothriums. One of the most

striking and important winter-flowering shrubs, Viburnum x bodnantense pictured right, was developed at Bodnant, and bears its Latinized name in recognition. Fabulous herbaceous borders and outstanding autumn colour add to the scene.

ABOVE *Bodnant's famous Laburnum Arch in springtime.*

LEFT *Splendid views to the Carneddau mountains and Snowdonia National Park from one of the terraces at Bodnant.*

RIGHT *This terrace has a clear view; on page 37 you can see how it looks with sea fog in the distance.*

RIGHT *Multi-terraced garden with the triangular house roof window making the most of the views of the planted levels.*

Making a level with water

Terraces in a sloping garden usually have a hard surface (that is, one you can stand on), but a pond can be laid level and set within the slope at one point and raised or supported at another. The surface of the water will find its own level and give the viewer – especially from a raised vantage point – the impression of a flat 'terrace'. The pond could be surrounded with rustic stonework (as seen in the picture), or a more formal paved edge. Depending on the space, the gradient and cost, there could be all manner of water accessories, such as fountains, cascades, bubble pools, and so on.

Chapter 6

CONTAINER GARDENS

Pots, troughs, tubs, urns, vases, hanging baskets, window boxes and even growing bags can all be used to convert a good garden into a great garden. The first five can be positioned on any hard surface. Hanging baskets and window boxes, by definition, should be attached to buildings or vertical walls. These will raise the colour level, but you must ensure that salt-tolerant plants are chosen.

RIGHT *View of Ishbel McWhirter's beautiful container garden, overlooking the Menai Strait, Anglesey, North Wales.*

Getting the best from containers

PLANTED CONTAINERS are at their most dramatic when used for seasonal displays of tender annuals (mainly bedding plants) and bulbs. When in full flowering glory, they make wonderful focal points. They are, of course, ideal for standing on a patio, path, driveway or next to a door, but they can also look very good when stood in borders. When plants in a tub are at their prettiest, the tub can be situated in a dull border and raised slightly on blocks. For a month or two, it can transform that part of the garden.

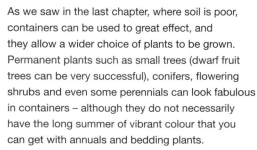

ABOVE *Gazanias make a hot and colourful summer splash in terracotta pots.*

As we saw in the last chapter, where soil is poor, containers can be used to great effect, and they allow a wider choice of plants to be grown. Permanent plants such as small trees (dwarf fruit trees can be very successful), conifers, flowering shrubs and even some perennials can look fabulous in containers – although they do not necessarily have the long summer of vibrant colour that you can get with annuals and bedding plants.

The main pitfall of containers is in the planting and maintenance of them. With the exception of vegetable plots and bedding displays, most areas of the garden need planting once and can then be left for a long time, often many years, before they need replanting. Flower containers require planting up on a seasonal basis. This can be minimized if you are growing specimen perennials, shrubs or trees in the containers, but even then it is often desirable to grow some temporary colour in and around the base. Then there is the maintenance of the containers – and this really comes down to one thing: watering (see page 87).

Lastly, in a coastal garden, you must also take account of the wind. In very exposed conditions, it is a good idea to weigh down containers by placing rocks or bricks in the base before potting, or putting heavy stones on the surface if high winds are forecast.

RIGHT *Winter pansies in containers can give some welcome colour during the colder months.*

ABOVE *Coastal regions are usually fairly frost-free, but when frosts do occur the results can be devastating for both plant and container.*

Terracotta containers can look wonderful in a Mediterranean-style setting. Check when buying them that they are frost-hardy, otherwise even a few short, cold spells can be sufficient to cause the clay to splinter into fragments.

In the case of hanging baskets, wire is the traditional type used; the soil within is kept in place using a basket liner. Sphagnum moss can be used for lining baskets, however, harvesting sphagnum from a natural habitat can harm indigenous wildlife, so it is better to use fabric liners in green, brown or black, which do the job just as well. If you do use moss, make sure that you line the basket discreetly with polythene as well, otherwise both the moss and the compost can fall out, especially if helped by visiting birds wanting to supplement their nests.

Plastic baskets are also available. These have filled-in sides and in many ways they are easier to manage. To start with, they dry out less quickly, and some types have a built-in water reservoir or tray to make the chore of watering less frequent. The basket you choose should have holes in the sides in order for trailing plants to be positioned.

Finally there are window boxes. Traditionally these were always of solid wood and very often made bespoke, for whichever window they were to adorn. Mass-produced plastic window boxes are cheaper, lightweight and available in various sizes; you can also buy sets consisting of the box, a water tray to avoid dripping and the all-important brackets for fixing to the wall.

As mentioned earlier – but we will reiterate it anyway – containers of any description should be anchored or weighted if they are likely to move in high winds. With hanging baskets and window boxes this is particularly important as, if they fall from a height, they can cause considerable damage. Brackets should be checked for stability and strength regularly.

LEFT *Careful planting of succulents around an old chair or something similar can create a picturesque Mediterranean scene.*

MATERIALS AND STYLES

Containers can be made from wood, terracotta, reconstituted stone, moulded resin and plastic. The latter are the cheapest and can be rather garish so choose what you want carefully.

Wooden containers can look very good and fit well in a coastal garden with decking or other whitewashed and maritime themes. But as with wooden furniture (see page 38), the wood used in containers may be prone to rotting caused by the constant salt-spray.

HOW TO PLANT UP CONTAINERS

When planting hardy plants into a container, it is a good idea to get the container into its final position before you start. This saves having to move it after it is planted, when it will be very heavy. If it is springtime and you are planting tender subjects for a summer outside, you may wish to do the planting in a greenhouse or shed, and to keep the planted container under cover for a week or two. This will give the tender plants time to establish and become stronger, and it will also allow time for the weather to warm up. Gradually acclimatize the plants to outside conditions, particularly if you will be placing them somewhere that is exposed to wind.

Planting pots, tubs, urns and vases

Start by putting some coarse material, such as broken flowerpots, pea gravel or washed stones, into the base of the container. You do not want to completely block the drainage hole in the bottom of the pot (and if there are no drainage holes, then you should drill some), but you do need to allow excess water to be able to escape.

Fill the tub two-thirds full with compost, firming it as you go. Use a loam-based compost, as this is longer-lasting than peat- or coir-based composts. These latter types will do quite well, but they are prone to quicker drying in warm weather. Check whether the compost has slow-release fertilizer added to it – many new brands of shop-bought compost have this included. It gets your plants off to a good start, but you will need to supplement the feed during the growing season. If there is no fertilizer already incorporated, you should add your own at this time.

A consistently moist compost throughout the growing season is important, for if compost is allowed to dry out the plants will not be able to suck up what they need to survive (let alone thrive). Water-retaining gels are being used more these days by environmentally conscious water-saving gardeners to solve this problem. They are sold as dry polymer granules, which are mixed with the compost at planting time; some composts now include granules as standard.

These granules absorb moisture and turn into a gel, swelling to many times their own weight. They release moisture to plants over many months and even seasons. Plants that benefit most from such

gels are those that grow rapidly and are planted in light, open compost, from which moisture quickly evaporates.

The best plants to put into a tub already come in pots. Remove the pots and set out the plants in the tub where they are to go. As a guide, placing one plant in the centre and four or five around the edge of a tub 12in (30cm) across is about right. Set each plant so that the surface of its root ball is 1in (2.5cm) below the rim of the tub. Fill around the root balls with more compost, firm gently and water well.

Throughout the growing season, and longer if you have potted up shrubs or perennials, you will be able to add temporary colour in the form of bedding plants, annuals and bulbs. This means that you can have the same permanent planting from year to year, but the supplementary colour can change on an annual basis. This makes for an interesting and ever-changing garden.

RIGHT *This typical pool and patio (in southern Turkey) would look stark without its arrangement of decorative containers.*

RIGHT *Using a backdrop for a collection of containers can make the most of their colour and form.*

BELOW *Formally clipped plants help to give structure in a garden.*

BELOW *Children's buckets and spades hanging on a tree in a seaside garden in Dorset, UK, make a great and unusual feature.*

ABOVE AND RIGHT
Archetypal French hanging baskets adorn a balcony.

Planting hanging baskets

Start by making sure that your basket is stable. Use the chains to hang it from a greenhouse support or wall bracket, or remove them and place the basket to sit within the rim of a large pot.

Place the liner in the basket, making sure that it fits snugly, then put a circle of plastic in the base to act as a water reserve. Begin filling your basket with compost; if your basket allows you to plant through its sides, only fill it halfway for the moment.

The taller plants should be placed firmly in the centre, to create a good structure. Put some trailing plants in the sides; cut holes in the liner if there aren't any, then push the rootballs through the hole from the outside, pulling them through gently.

Some composts have feeds added, which last just a few weeks (check the packaging) – these will need liquid-feeding later in the season. If your compost does not have feed in it, add slow-release fertilizer. Add some more of the compost, then the small plants can go in. Give the basket a good water to settle in the plants.

Until the basket is ready to go outside, it is best to hang it in a greenhouse, a warm, well-lit conservatory or a bright room.

Planting window boxes

The process of planting a window box – which should be carried out after the box has been put into position and secured – is similar to that of the pots and tubs discussed on page 84.

Smaller and trailing plants are particularly appropriate to window-box schemes. Permanent plants, such as shrubs and perennials, are less successful in window boxes because they tend to get rather large and are usually only at their best for a short period. When these plants are not in season, the window box will not be very attractive.

Mostly when you see such woody plants as variegated ivies, heaths and heathers (forms of *Erica carnea*), *Euonymus* and other evergreens, and dwarf conifers, they are used more as temporary infills of foliage, particularly during the winter months when there is less colour to be had with flowering plants. These woody plants do not mind cold winter temperatures and are usually fine even in exposed coastal situations.

Watering plants in containers

During the warmer months, container plants need checking daily for water requirements – even twice daily in very hot weather – as they can dry out rapidly. Hanging baskets, especially, are notorious for this. Potted plants need watering all year round, except in freezing conditions. In winter, the rain may do it for you, but keep checking because foliage can act like an umbrella, or a wall can create a dry spot. It is best to water in the early morning or evening when evaporation rates are at their lowest.

By mid summer, hanging baskets are full of plants and use a lot of water. Even worse, they tend to hang by sunny walls, and the heat that the walls reflect makes them dry out even more. So anything that you can do to keep them moist is worthwhile.

Use the retaining gels in these for a constant supply of moisture. Use rainwater from a tank or water butt for irrigating mature container plants, but use tap water for seedlings and young plants, which are more delicate and more prone to infection from the impurities and bacteria present in rainwater.

The best way to water is with a watering can fitted with a rose spray, which distributes water evenly. If you do not have a rose spray, place a piece of slate or old crock in the corner of the container, tilted downwards, and gently pour water on to it. This method prevents soil compaction and gives an even distribution of water. Ideally, repeat this in each corner.

Hanging baskets are notoriously awkward to water – and cause sleeves and arms to get wet in the process! It's worth investing in a special extension hose and hooked watering lance so that you do not have to hold up heavy watering cans. With these you will also be able to direct water more easily to where it is needed.

Automatic watering systems are available but expensive. However, they are very effective and water-efficient, and can be regarded as essential if your garden-by-the-sea is a second home or holiday home and you are absent for long periods. You preset the times when you want the system to start and stop, and in the more sophisticated versions you can even determine how much water should be used. It is a good idea to make sure that the system is working properly even if you are away – ask a friend or neighbour to look in to check. Failure of the system could mean an expensive array of dead plants on your return.

RIGHT *Well-planted hanging baskets and containers not only look good, but will also attract plenty of customers!*

RIGHT *Watering lances or wands make the job of watering hanging baskets much easier.*

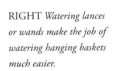

PATIOS AND CONTAINERS

If your coastal garden has views of the sea, you owe it to yourself to, wherever possible, create a patio area where you can relax and take in these views. But even if your garden is more enclosed, an area to entertain and to sit and read or relax with a drink is just as important.

Equally important, however, is the use of plants on and around the patio. Just imagine how intensely boring a patio would be if it had no plants at all on it. You would be missing out on the colour, the form and in many cases the scents of plants, and you would be surrounded by stark paving and walling. It would be like (we imagine) a prison courtyard!

With a patio made of flagstones, concrete or some other such hard surface, it is not easy to find or create suitable pockets of soil into which plants can be set. Therefore, in most cases, you will find that a patio becomes a hard surface for containers – tubs, troughs, planters, urns, vases – and do not forget hanging baskets and window boxes set on the walls for good measure.

RIGHT *Enhance patios and barbecue areas by 'dressing' them with attractive plants in containers.*

BELOW *A circular, or 'island' bed, within patio brickwork.*

Strategic use of containers

When composing a group of containers, it usually pays to put the most dramatic plants in the most strategic position. This could be at the end of a run (as seen in the picture, right, where coastal-tolerant exotic and succulent plants have been lined up); in a more symmetrical grouping, the most strategic place is likely to be near the centre.

If you are building a display with a 'crescendo' towards the centre, it is often a good idea to exaggerate the height of the centrepiece plant, by raising it on blocks, bricks and so on. These will often be hidden by smaller containers in the front or by trailing stems and foliage. Or, you can create an effective display by putting the largest plant at the back – preferably an evergreen so that you do not have to keep changing it as its appearance alters – then range the remaining pots down in size, making a tiered arrangement. Of course, the main benefit of having containers in a garden is so they can be quickly planted, or moved into a better position, when they are filled with seasonal colour.

ABOVE *Tiered arrangements, with the largest pots at the back, work particularly well in the corner of a patio or balcony, as the display fans out towards the front.*

PLAN: CONTAINER GARDEN

A　Summerhouse
B　Steps
C　Croquet lawn
D　Deck area
E　Table and chairs
F　Barbecue
G　Low screening plants
H　Palms
I　Tree
J　Palms
K　Mixed containers
L　Mixed containers
M　Bamboos in containers
N　Palms
O　Cliff
P　Existing hedge

The design for this garden (which was actually set on a clifftop) involved a long lawn and a deck at the far end, which was the part of the garden that receives most sunlight. Mixed containers form a major part of the plantings on the left and right of the garden as you look down it, and of course the entertainment area on the deck would be enhanced with container plantings also.

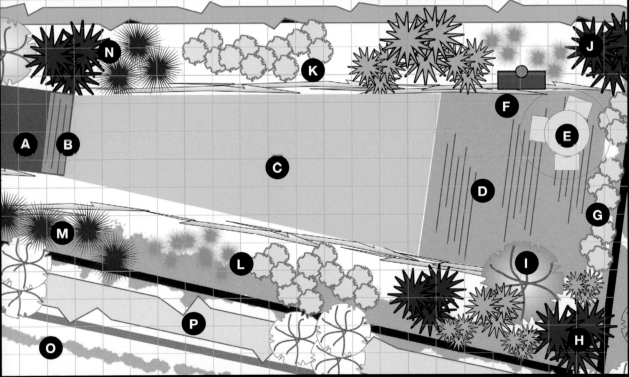

Madeira Botanical Gardens

Container and bedding plants have become something of a feature at the island of Madeira's most treasured and certainly most famous tourist attraction. Within the Botanical Gardens – an area of 95,500 sq yd (80,000m²) – one encounters a fascinating collection of more than 2,500 plant species (see page 188 for details). With its location in the impressive amphitheatre of Funchal, Madeira's capital, the Botanical Gardens provides its visitors with panoramic views over the mountainous backdrop, the city below and its bay with the deep blue waters of the Atlantic.

Two hundred years ago there were already those who dreamed of establishing a botanical garden. The wonderful climate and the island's fertile soils were excellent reasons for pioneers such as J.R. Theodore Vogel in 1841, Frederico Weltwitsch in 1852 and the naturalist Baron Castello de Paiva in 1855, to pave the way for the gardens seen today.

In 1881 the Reid family (well known for their distinguished Reid's Hotel in Funchal) constructed the Quinta do Bom Sucesso. In the past century it was acquired by the Regional Government, and the Botanical Gardens were created on its grounds and opened to the public in 1960.

ABOVE *A collection of tropical foliage plants in containers, including* Aeonium 'Zwartkop' AGM, *variegated* Ficus benjamina *and* Agave.

Plants to see at the Madeira Botanical Gardens

Arboretum: *This contains an assortment of species, including ginkgos, magnolias, cedars, palms, snowball trees, pines, jacarandas, oaks, Ficus, stinkwoods, laurels, dragon trees, Eucalyptus, cassias and acacias.*

Succulents: *Within the gardens you will find cacti, aloes, agaves, yuccas, euphorbias, sempervivums, crassulas, and so on. These plants are native to the arid or semi-desert regions of Asia, Africa and North, South and Central America, but they also thrive in this warm yet maritime environment.*

Medicinal and aromatic plants: *Because of its geographical isolation in the Atlantic Ocean, Madeira is a centre of medicinal plant diversity, with a richness of endemic flora.*

The authorized medicinal flora of Madeira is composed of 259 species, and all of them are good candidates for coastal gardens within the same temperature range. Noteworthy plants include: Acanthus mollis, Aeonium glandulosum, Aeonium glutinosum, Bidens pilosa, Borago officinalis, Chamaemelum nobile *var.* discoideum, Echium nervosum, Euphorbia platiphylla, Helichrysum melaleucum, Helichrysum obconicum, Hypericum glandulosum, Rubus bollei, Rumex maderensis, Sambucus lanceolata, Scilla maderensis, Sedum farinosum, Teucrium betonicum, Thymus caespititius, Trifolium squamosum *and* Vaccinium padifolium.

LEFT *Amazing geometric shapes are created in the annual bedding schemes; they are based on traditional island colours.*

RIGHT *Roof gardens, Singapore, where even mature palms and trees are grown in containers.*

RIGHT *Aloes and aoniums make great companion succulent plants in terracotta pots.*

Olive trees

Olive trees (Olea europaeus) have been cultivated for centuries. Both their fruits and their timber have been vital to the survival of whole communities over the years. And, being native to hot countries, the trees provide shade to people and animals that has been no less important.

Olives grow very well in coastal regions, as long as they are sheltered from the strongest winds and are given plenty of direct sunlight. Evergreen, the beautiful tiny, grey-green leaves seem to shimmer in the sunlight. Old trees develop a venerable, gnarled appearance; plants can live for many hundreds of years, and they seem to remain productive for all of their lives.

These trees have become very popular in the cooler, temperate gardens – and streets – in northern European countries, where they are grown for their appearance rather than for their fruits. However, some street trees in central London are regularly 'harvested' by passers-by – although the fruits are usually completely unpalatable!

Chapter 7

THE PRODUCTIVE COASTAL GARDEN

It is quite possible to grow a wide range of fruits and vegetables in containers for siting on the deck or patio, but what about an area of the coastal garden dedicated to food crops? How can a productive kitchen garden be incorporated into a decorative garden, and can it be that productive anyway, bearing in mind the constant wind and salty air?

RIGHT *Most short-term vegetable crops can grow perfectly well in coastal gardens. Longer-term fruiting trees and shrubs may need some protection.*

Maximizing fruit and vegetables

GARDENS A FEW MILES from the sea can generally accommodate a wide range of fruits and vegetables. But most vegetables and soft fruit will grow well only in a light, open, sunny site that is well sheltered from the wind. Top or tree fruits are hardier, but they will not appreciate a garden that is too exposed either.

Wind and salt can also cause serious damage, from which plants may not recover completely, include flagging and discoloured leaves and limp stems, and haphazard flowering with little or no setting. Sometimes, for no apparent reason, the swelling of fruits and pods seems to stop. If these types of severe symptoms appear, then it is best not to grow these crops again, but to experiment with alternatives that might be more suitable.

Irrigate the vegetable plot with rainwater or tap water whenever it is required, but when you do make sure that the soil around the roots of the plants is thoroughly soaked, rather than just giving them a daily splash-about.

With regard to watering fruit trees and shrubs, always water in at planting time, and check regularly for dryness for the first year. In the case of bush fruits (blackcurrant, red currant, white currant, and gooseberry), it is usually advised to apply water at around 4½ gallons per sq yd (20 litres per m²) every 10 days during dry periods from flowering until harvest time. With cane fruits, keep the water off the canes themselves, to minimize fungal problems.

SEAWEED AND SHELLS: NATURAL RESOURCES

Seaweed makes a good, bulky manure, and there is no doubt that liberal use of this (or well-rotted compost or manure) is an essential feature of kitchen gardening.

Unfortunately seaweed does attract flies, which will invade the house if windows are open, so it is best collected and hauled in winter, when there are fewer flies, and the seaweed itself is more plentiful. Also check with your local authority that seaweed harvesting is permitted.

Once home, it can then be spread on the soil, to be dug in when partially dried. Alternatively, it can be added to the compost heap, mixed with other green material, then covered with lawn clippings to encourage decay without the flies.

On many beaches seaweed comes mixed with broken shells. These contain a high proportion of calcium and, if spread on the soil in quantity, can have the effect of raising the pH level. This is usually most welcome in the vegetable garden, as the pH tends to drop as calcium is leached from the soil through continual cultivation.

RIGHT *Seaweed is a great natural resource for coastal gardeners.*

BELOW *Chives are a useful herb, and they also bring a welcome bit of colour into the garden.*

HERBS FOR THE COASTAL GARDEN

Most of the plants we know as culinary (as well as medicinal and cosmetic) herbs originally came from dry areas around the Mediterranean Sea and the Middle East. In these places, the soils are often very poor or very sandy, or maybe both, so herbs are usually quite a good choice for seaside gardens in temperate countries.

Unfortunately, gardeners living in countries such as Canada and Scandinavia that have low winter temperatures usually have a little more trouble keeping herbs growing outdoors the year round. However, provided that winter temperatures do not fall much below 5°F (-15°C), then perennial culinary herbs are usually successful when grown within a few miles of the sea.

Members of the onion family, such as garlic (*Allium sativum*) and chives (*A. schoenoprasum*), do well near the coast. In temperate countries garlic may be left to overwinter in the ground as a perennial. Chives are familiar and useful herb onions, grown for their leaves. Both are drought-resistant and dislike waterlogged soil.

Mint (*Mentha* spp) is one of the most familiar of herbs, present in most gardens, whether or not there is a dedicated herb-growing area. There are many to choose from, all with subtly different flavours and aromas, and most will be happy close to the sea. Spearmint (*M. spicata*) is the type commonly used in chewing gum, and it goes well with new potatoes. But so does peppermint (*M.* x *piperita*) and applemint (*M. suaveolens*).

Mints thrive in full sun and ordinary soil, and they are drought-resistant. They can also become somewhat invasive if they are happy where they are, so it is a good idea to keep them from taking over the garden by planting them in containers sunk to their rims in the ground. Repot and thin out the congested pots every two or three years.

There are many forms of tarragon, but to most cooks the best type is the authentic, or French, tarragon (*Artemesia dracunculus*). It has narrow, elongated glossy leaves which have a subtle, slightly aniseed-like flavour.

Oregano (*Origanum vulgare*) is an untidy-looking plant with white or pinkish flowers; a much more attractive form, 'Aureum', has golden leaves.

Sage (*Salvia officinalis*) and thyme (*Thymus* spp) both adapt well to coastal situations, as do feverfew (*Tanacetum parthenium*), sweet woodruff (*Galium odoratum*) and hyssop (*Hyssopus officinalis*).

Lavender (*Lavandula* spp), catmint (*Nepeta* spp), rue (*Ruta graveolens*) and tansy (*Tanacetum vulgare*) all have culinary applications, but are probably best known for their medicinal properties.

GROWING FRUIT

Soft fruit

These fruits are adversely affected by the wind, so make sure that some shelter is provided. In all but the most exposed of conditions, strawberries grow close enough to the ground to avoid any serious damage occuring to the fruit.

Blackcurrants, gooseberries, blackberries, loganberries and the other so-called hybrid berries (tayberry, sunberry, dewberry and so on) are damaged to some degree by constant winds, and raspberries and red and white currants do not cope at all in windy conditions.

There are two types of raspberry: those that fruit in the summer and those that are ready in the autumn and even into early winter. The summer varieties have quite a short season; however, they do produce high yields. The autumn types, on the other hand, will bear fruits from the end of summer through to the first frosts.

Problems associated with coastal gardens and raspberries are that these fruits do not like light, dry soils (they need a really moisture-retentive soil packed full of goodness, from well-rotted manure to garden compost), and they can be prone to greymould disease, which is often worse in damp seaside conditions.

Loganberries and strawberries are also prone to greymould. In the case of the latter it is therefore better to choose a variety, such as 'Pantagruella', which has smaller leaves and where the fruits stand well above them. In general they prefer a warm, sunny, sheltered position; this kind of position usually guarantees the best-flavoured berries.

Tree fruit

Any of the fruits mentioned below can be grown successfully, but they are likely to have reduced crops as compared to similar trees growing inland. Yet again it is the wind that causes most problems.

New fruit trees should be planted as young as possible, as older or larger trees often have great difficulty in producing an adequate root system to hold the head of branches, leaves and – hopefully – heavy fruit crops in windy conditions. Regardless of age, good staking is crucial in the formative years. It is important also to make sure that the ties are secure to prevent chafing of the stem or trunk in the consistently windy weather.

Shelter, facilitated by windbreaks or fences, is the key to success. If flowering coincides with strong winds, the flight of pollinating insects will be reduced and less fruit will be the result. Similarly, if autumn gales come before ripening and picking (as they invariably do with the later-maturing varieties of apples and pears), windfalls will be more plentiful and storable crops will be diminished.

Even earlier in the summer, the developing fruits may be bruised by being banged against each other. Even the rasp of leaves can damage the skins of some fruits (including members of the plum, cherry and peach family).

Finally, there is the problem of scab and canker diseases, which are worse in the humid atmosphere near the sea. Scab attacks leaves and branches, and spoils the appearance of the fruit; canker kills twigs and branches, and even whole trees if left to spread. Both diseases can be controlled by spraying, but it must be thorough and, in moist

LEFT *The Karikari Estate Winery, close to the sea in the north of New Zealand, produces high-quality wines.*

ABOVE *Figs, along with mulberries, do well in coastal areas.*

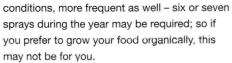

conditions, more frequent as well – six or seven sprays during the year may be required; so if you prefer to grow your food organically, this may not be for you.

If you are prepared to go without ornamental climbers on your house or boundary walls, you may like to consider trained forms of fruit. Apples, pears, cherries, peaches and plums can all be very successful when grown against wires. If grown facing the sun they will certainly be warm, and usually sheltered from the wind too, but you will probably need to pay attention to watering during the warmer months.

LEFT *(Clockwise from top left) Apples, pears, plums and gages often benefit from the warmer conditions found by the coast.*

GROWING VEGETABLES

In general, vegetables grown in a coastal garden are likely to be far more successful than fruiting crops. With a little attention to detail, there is no reason why you should not have a full and productive vegetable garden. There are, however, a few points to bear in mind with certain crops.

Legumes

The 'pod and seed' vegetables can roughly be divided into those that produce edible seeds (peas and broad beans) and those that are grown for their edible pods (runner beans and mangetout). The pods of French or dwarf beans can be eaten, or just the seeds from within them.

Runner beans need to be well staked and tied, otherwise they can be brought down swiftly in a windy garden. Dwarf varieties are especially suited to coastal gardens, as they are less affected by wind than the taller climbers. An alternative is not to stake the beans at all, but to allow them to run along the ground. The crops are just as heavy, but the beans are not straight, and picking them by working your way through and between plants can become tiresome.

Planning ahead is the key to getting a good runner bean crop, as the soil should be prepared several months beforehand, with masses of well-rotted compost or manure dug deeply.

Similarly, dwarf garden peas can be grown along the ground. They are often described as round or wrinkled – not a precise description of the shape of the pea, but more as a way of classifying them as hardy (round for autumn sowing) or tender (wrinkled for spring sowing).

Mangetout and sugar snap peas are bred to be eaten whole, pod and all. Mangetout (French for 'eat all') are ready when the pods are flat, before the peas inside have developed. Sugar snaps should be eaten once the peas are fully developed and the pods have rounded out.

ABOVE *Vegetables are best grown behind a shelter belt.*

RIGHT *Onions thrive in coastal conditions.*

BELOW *Vegetables from the beach – samphire (left) and sea kale (right).*

Brassicas

These include such luminaries as cabbage (spring, summer, autumn and winter varieties), cauliflower, broccoli and calabrese, Brussels sprouts, kale, turnips and Swedes. Being root crops, and therefore very different in habit and shape to their 'green' cousins, the last two are not usually thought of as brassicas. But they are, and therefore just as susceptible to all of the foibles and weaknesses of the main members of the family – such as vulnerability to the fungal disease clubroot and being prone to attack by birds.

It is often desirable to earth up the taller winter brassicas, such as sprouting and winter broccoli and Brussels sprouts. At planting time the young plants should be set in a shallow drill drawn by a hoe. They are supported as the soil is levelled around them and in subsequent hoeing.

After this they are further supported by earthing up, as you would do with potatoes. The shallow ridge and furrow created against and next to the plants creates not only support for the stems, but also a certain amount of drainage.

Vegetables over winter

Winter lettuce, winter spinach, autumn-sown broad beans and peas, and spring onions can all be blown to pieces where strong winds sweep across exposed gardens. Shelter belts, windbreaks and fences can all save crops from devastation, but you may also wish to make use of garden frames, cloches or even polytunnels (if you have the space) to protect your plants.

LEFT *Ornamental winter cabbages add a welcome splash of colour.*

RIGHT *The extensive walled kitchen garden at Inverewe, Scotland.*

Chapter 8

TROPICAL AND EXOTIC-LOOKING GARDENS

The perceived image of the tropics is of hot, steamy jungles comprising large-leaved palms and trees clad with orchids and bromeliads, all striving to reach the little bit of light that manages to fight its way through the high tree canopy. With deserts we have visions of dry, wide-open, rolling sand ridges and strategically placed cacti, succulents and boulders. Beautiful images, but can we re-create them in a coastal garden?

RIGHT Tree ferns, bananas and Japanese acers at
Abbotsbury Subtropical Gardens, England.

Creating a rainforest garden

THE IDEA OF capturing the sights and smells of a rainforest or jungle can be very appealing. This style of garden should be free of conformity and man-made restrictions – experiment and let your imagination take over. Living near the sea poses one or two issues, but a jungle coastal garden is entirely possible. However, cramming it into a tiny garden might be rather more of a challenge!

In recent years, garden centres have increased the range of plant styles stocked, with an ever-growing array of unusual imports from foreign nurseries. The choice, therefore, is wide, but the keys to succeeding with them lie in reducing their exposure to the elements and not allowing them to languish in icy, muddy soil for long periods in winter. Heavy rains and waterlogged roots can be much more serious than salt in the air or even occasional extreme cold spells.

Of course, you do not need to devote your whole garden to the rainforest. Carefully placing even a single specimen of a large exotic-looking plant can dramatically alter the look. Painting fences and other structures in new colours, or using colourful 'accessories' such as ceramic pots and jars, or interesting driftwood, or even ethnic artefacts (such as totem poles or some other carved items) can further enhance the tropical look.

Finally, if space is limited, you can quite easily create a tropical look by using containers. An *Agave* in a large urn, or a banana in a patio pot, can give any deck or patio a beautiful tropical makeover.

ABOVE *Sales of exotic and tropical plants at Abbotsbury Subtropical Gardens, England.*

LEFT *This secluded Zen garden in the Bay of Islands, New Zealand, has a very tropical feel.*

PLANTS TO CHOOSE

Grasses, bamboos, bananas, cannas, gingers, palms … the list of plants suited to jungle-like situations is huge. Most will tolerate some salty air, but, if you live right on the beach, you should maybe stick to growing grasses and bamboos.

Annuals usually do quite well in coastal gardens, as they last only a single year and are unlikely to suffer from long-lasting wind or salt damage. The choice is somewhat limited when it comes to large, exotic-looking annuals, as most are grown for their flower and colour impact. Watch out, however, for three excellent plants. First is the tampala (*Amaranthus tricolor*), which is great for subtropical bedding schemes and comes in stunning reds, maroons and oranges.

The second annual is the castor oil plant (*Ricinus communis*). It is a magnificent, bold, foliage plant with large hand-shaped leaves of a greenish copper, with red veins and stalks. It makes a bold statement in the border, but be aware that its seeds are poisonous and plants should not be grown where children can get to them.

The third annual is the tobacco flower (*Nicotiana sylvestris*), which has delicate, white, tubular flowers that are highly scented, particularly in the evening. It sometimes overwinters like a perennial in sheltered, mild gardens, but it is never as good, nor as vigorous, in subsequent years.

The *Aeonium*, although a succulent, is actually an exotic, lush-looking perennial or small shrub with glossy, soft leaf rosettes. These plants adore being close to the sea and loathe being in cold, shady places in a heavy soil. Another exotic-looking succulent for the maritime garden is *Beschorneria yuccoides*. An evergreen perennial, it produces rosettes of large, fleshy, sword-shaped leaves and pinky red flowers on long stalks.

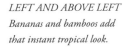

ABOVE LEFT Aloes and yuccas create an exotic feel in this contemporary garden at Hot Water Bay on the Coromandel Peninsula, New Zealand.

ABOVE Tree ferns and gunneras at Abbotsbury Subtropical Gardens, England.

LEFT Aloes make great container plants.

ABOVE RIGHT The Pohutukawi tree – also called the New Zealand Christmas tree – can be found along many shorelines in New Zealand.

RIGHT AND BELOW RIGHT Cordylines and aloes thriving in the climate of New Zealand

LEFT AND ABOVE LEFT Bananas and bamboos add that instant tropical look.

LEFT *Minimal planting of a specimen* Aloe speciosa *makes a stunning architectural statement.*

RIGHT *Cacti in the botanical garden in Singapore, Southeast Asia.*

Creating a desert garden

BELOW Aloe polyphylla *forms a perfect spiral – sometimes clockwise; sometimes anticlockwise.*

ENTHUSIASTS OF CACTI and succulents often display them in pots and keep them under cover. They make marvellous plants for greenhouses, conservatories, sun rooms and bright, sunny windowsills. In the garden, however, they are a very different proposition and can make a dramatic statement if grown successfully.

Naturally, many succulents come from the dry areas of the tropics and subtropics, where high temperatures and low rainfall have forced them to develop ways of collecting and storing water in order to survive long, dry periods. Succulents also occur as inhabitants of coastal areas, as well as on saltpans, which are exposed to high levels of dissolved minerals.

In gardens, these tender plants are striking and easy to care for and will tolerate the hottest and driest of summers – and, gratifyingly, without the need for endless watering.

The key to succeeding with succulents, as with the rainforest plants, is to remember that they are generally tolerant of cold conditions, as long as they are dry. They will quickly perish if they are both cold and wet, so it is best to avoid growing them outside in low-lying areas. Think of the cactus-

strewn clifftops around much of the Mediterranean; the plants are fully exposed to the elements, but no water languishes around the roots.

Choose a sheltered part of your coastal garden; even better, take advantage of the microclimates in the garden by planting in the shelter of a sunny wall. Not only will this block the wind, but it will also retain some of the sun's daytime warmth into the nighttime. Walls also shelter plants from driving rain, so the soil tends to be drier here.

Plant out your subjects in mid-spring, so that they have as long a time as possible to develop a good root system before the following winter arrives. Good drainage is important, so add plenty of grit to planting holes.

There are a few tricks to protect plants in really cold areas. The first rule is to keep them in a container and bring them inside for the winter. Secondly, you should have plenty of cuttings as a backup. And thirdly, if the plants need to stay outside for winter, you can use horticultural fleece, bubble wrap plastic, or paper, cloth or straw as a temporary blanket covering for the plants during cold spells. This should only be temporary, however, as cacti and succulents will suffer if excluded from light and fresh air for more than a few days at a

LEFT, ABOVE AND RIGHT *Cacti look best when grouped together, although their flowers often come out at night or last for only one day.*

time. Also, if you use bubble wrap, remove it every morning to get rid of condensation on the inside, as if the plants are in contact with this for a long time they will eventually rot.

The most effective 'desert gardens' use lots of sand or gravel, with various cacti and succulents planted in drifts, coming out of the desert-like surface. Such plants associate well with a whole range of other dramatic architectural plants such as phormiums, bamboos, ornamental grasses and other spiky plants, to create a really unusual garden.

Weeding around cacti is always going to be a problem, as you do not want to get too close to their spines. Therefore it is best to lay down a weed-smothering membrane over the bed or border, cut holes in it to plant your plants, then cover the membrane with either gravel or sand.

PLANTS TO CHOOSE

The hardiest cacti and succulents will survive outdoors all year round in the most protected of sites. Look for *Agave parryi*, a compact plant with grey-blue leaves some 12in (30cm) long. *Aloe striatula* has tall, dark green leaf rosettes and produces tall, orange-red flower spikes; *A. aristata,* on the other hand, is not so tall and forms a dense cluster of stemless rosettes.

Delosperma cooperi is a succulent perennial whose spreading, fleshy leaves will die back in a cold winter, but reappear in spring. All throughout the growing season it produces lilac daisy flowers.

Carpobrutus deliciosus has long, greyish-green leaves on creeping stems and pink-purple flowers, with edible, spherical fig-like fruits.

In addition there are some forms of *Echinocereus, Lampranthus, Opuntia, Sedum, Sempervivum* and *Yucca* that can withstand winters outdoors in temperate countries – as long as there is some protection from the cold and wet.

LEFT *Although cacti and succulents can withstand low temperatures, they need extra protection if it is wet and cold.*

RIGHT *Agaves and aloes make good container specimens.*

WATER FEATURES AND DECKING

There is no doubt that one of the greatest joys in a garden is water. You just have to sit by a pool and spend a few minutes watching fish, frogs and the other forms of aquatic wildlife to feel immediately that there is peace in the world. If you have a pond and you have installed a pump, you can also gain from the relaxing sight and sound of a trickling fountain or a cascade of water tumbling over well-placed stone.

Just because your garden is near to the sea, and maybe even with a view of the sea as a feature, there is no reason why you should not enhance your gardening pleasure – and views – with some sort of freshwater feature.

Ponds in the formal style of a circle, square, rectangle or oval are, perhaps, the simplest you could choose. Informal ponds, in irregular shapes, are better placed in natural-looking or wild gardens.

You do not need to limit yourself to ground-based ponds. Water features can be raised, and they can include wall fountains, barrel containers, rockery cascades and even contemporary jets that 'spurt' dramatically from one 'reservoir' to another.

It is not compulsory, obviously, to edge your pond with wooden decking – but it does seem somehow fitting if the garden is close to the sea, and fairly essential if you want to create a garden with a maritime theme. Traditionally the decking is in natural wood tones but, as can be seen in some of the pictures on these pages, owners of wooden decking can experiment with colours.

RIGHT *Simple but well-constructed decking positioned next to or over still water can be most effective, and is arguably the most serene of situations.*

Timber decking

Decking creates a distinctive look in the garden and will make a refreshing change from ordinary paving. Narrow planks look best in a small or enclosed garden, but in a larger, more open area use a wider plank.

All timber used for decking should be thoroughly treated with a wood preservative. Some preservatives also come in a range of colours, including dark brown, black, grey, green, blue and various shades of red – but be careful if you choose the brighter colours, as you can easily 'overdo' it, with the result that the decking is gaudy and garish.

If you want your decking to have a long life, special pressure-treated timber is the best choice; however, the range of available colours is more limited. In some countries there are building codes and regulations that may have to be met. If in doubt, seek professional help with the design, even if you build and install it yourself.

ABOVE *A water pump positioned under a deck gives the effect of running water.*

PLAN: WATER AND DECKING GARDEN

A   Summerhouse
B   Deck
C   Table, chairs, parasol
D   Pond
E   Pebbles/shingle
F   Sleeper groins
G   Lobster pots
H   Mixed low shrubs
I   Large phormiums
J   Colourful perennials
K   Lobster pot
L   Palm
M   Shrubby pine
N   Mixed grasses
O   Water flow pump
P   Safety rope

This small seaside garden (inset picture) was created specifically to include water, planting and a deck area for relaxation. Groins, so much a feature of traditional coastlines, have been emulated using treated railway sleepers placed on end. The planting needs to be fairly dense, to provide plenty of interest, so for this reason you should not choose vigorous subjects, or you will be forever pruning or thinning out.

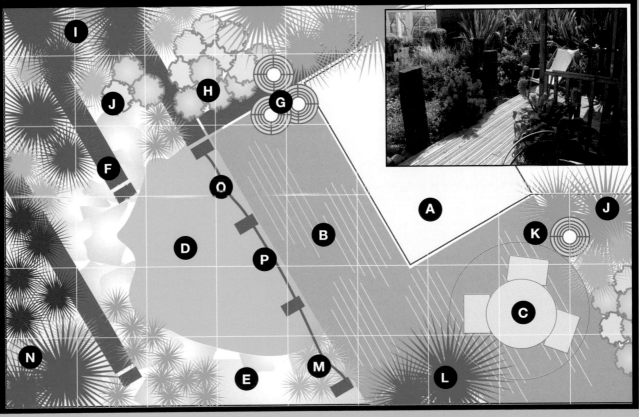

Brookgreen Gardens, South Carolina

Founded in 1931, Brookgreen Gardens are a spectacular part of South Carolina's coastal community. To start with they are simply enormous; then there is the zoo, and the fact that it is the first public sculpture garden in the US. Plus it boasts more than 20 water features, fountains, ponds and lakes.

Situated south of Myrtle Beach and north of Georgetown (see page 188 for details), the land surrounding the gardens is a mix of forested swamps, salt marsh, sandy ridges and fresh tidal swamps. The gardens have effectively preserved the natural heritage of the area, yet at the same time manage to offer the visitor stunning display gardens.

Also known as the Archer and Anna Hyatt Huntington Sculpture Garden, the area was first laid out by Anna Hyatt Huntington in the shape of a spread-wing butterfly. On entering the Diana Garden, the breadth of this magnificent place is fully revealed. The Live Oak Allee garden is framed by massive 250-year-old live oak trees that were planted in the early 1700s when the space was a thriving rice plantation.

One of the most recent gardens is also the most whimsical. The Fountain of the Muses Garden (pictured below), designed to display the sculpture of the same name, takes garden design to another level.

Aquatic plants

Only ponds and sizeable water features with areas of still water can really accommodate plants, for it is generally accepted that plants need room to develop, and relatively still (not persistently splashing) water.

Floating plants include the water hyacinth (Eichhornia crassipes) and water violet (Hottonia palustris). Duckweed (Lemna spp) and fairy moss (Azolla spp) are sometimes purposely introduced to a pond, but they can quickly form a carpet over the surface, blocking out light and debilitating submerged plants, fish and wildlife.

Then there are the flowering aquatic plants that grow in a depth of water. These include plants such as golden club (Orontium aquaticum), pickerel weed (Pontaderia cordata) and, of course, the many different forms of water lily. For lilies, consult a specialist to help you, as the range is so great and they do demand quite specific conditions.

Lastly, there are the marginal plants which grow in mud or containers at the edge of the pond. Familiar plants for this spot include the arum lily (Zantedeschia aethiopica), bog arum (Calla palustris) and cotton grass (Eriophorum angustifolium).

LEFT *A seaside show garden created specially for the Devon Air Ambulance, UK.*

RIGHT *Decking can, of course, be used in strips to make an attractive wooden walkway across a pond or water feature.*

Keeping pond fish

Once you have a pond installed, and filled with tap water, the urge to put some decorative freshwater fish in it straight away can be enormous. Resist it! A new pond must settle down, even for as long as six weeks, before fish should be introduced.

Whatever species or variety of fish you choose, you should know just how many fish, and of what size, your pond can accommodate safely. Allow 24sq in (155cm²) of water surface area per 1in (2.5cm) length of fish – excluding the tail! Once the calculation has been made, reduce it by 25 per cent, to allow for the fish to grow.

When selecting fish at the shop, follow these six rules:
1. The fish should look lively and be alert.
2. The fins should be well extended, not collapsed.
3. The scales on its body should all be present and intact.
4. The eyes should be clear.
5. The colouring(s) should be vivid and clear, not dull or cloudy.
6. The swimming technique of the fish should be considered – the fish should not be floating or sinking, rolling or losing balance.

Part Three

COASTAL
Plant Style

We have examined the reasons why people want to live by the coast
and also how they can create a garden to suit their lifestyle. We have
also examined some of the challenges of gardening by the sea.
But what about the plants? Which ones can grow where?

How to use hardiness zone maps

Before investing time, effort and, of course, money on new plant purchases, you should first understand your geographical location and what this means to the plants in your care. It is particularly important to have an appreciation of temperatures and the tolerance of plants to cold.

For many years the standard used in the United States has been the Harvard University-derived 'hardiness zones'. The original zone map was that of the United States, but it has been adapted for use in the UK and Europe. These maps enable gardeners to judge how plants will grow and thrive, wherever they live.

Certain plants – such as the tropical cannas and bananas from the West Indies or Mediterranean regions, or the cacti and succulents of Mexico and South America – are obvious plant choices if you live in these zones. But if you live in England, or anywhere else in Europe or North America, these maps are designed to help you to understand which plants will survive in your garden, with or without being cosseted.

Areas within the maps are colour-coded into 11 distinct zones. Plants mentioned in this part of the book will be given a zone reference from Z1 to Z11. Find your location on the maps, and you can then identify which zone your garden falls into. Do not forget to take into account that cities are warmer than rural locations, and that planting shelter belts of trees, or windbreaks, can dramatically improve conditions for plants.

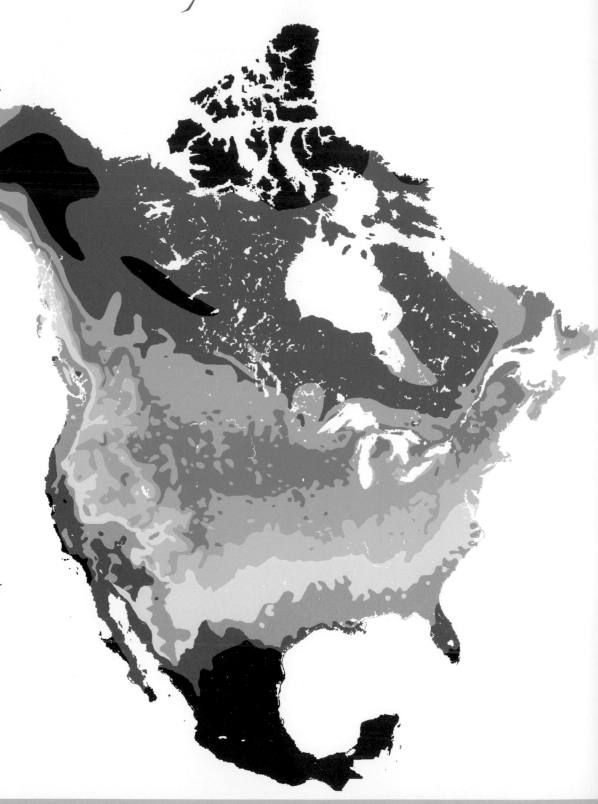

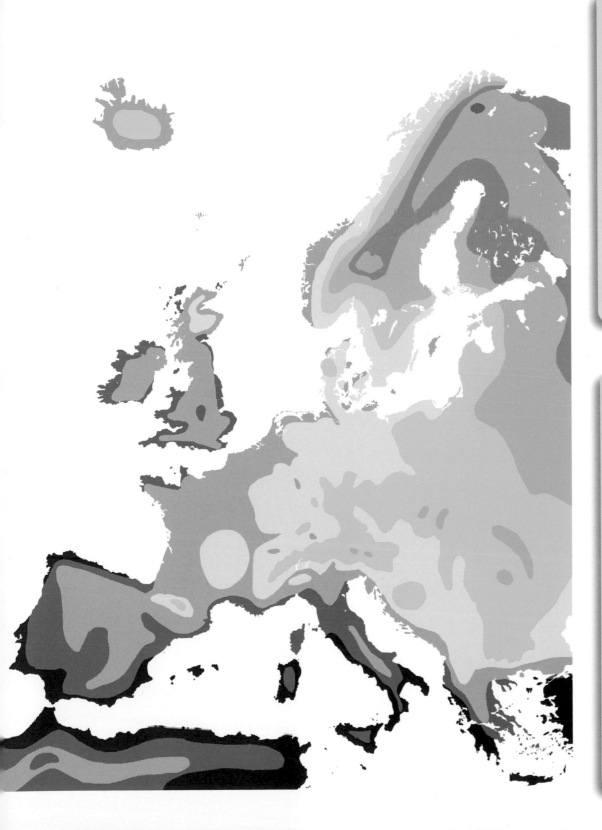

Throughout the directory section that follows, you will see the initials 'AGM' set after certain plants. This denotes that the plant in question has passed certain assessments carried out by experts under the auspices of the Royal Horticultural Society in the UK. Only plants with exceptionally good garden qualities can be given this special Award of Garden Merit, which gives you a degree of reassurance. All you have to do is choose a plant that in right for the situation and care for it properly.

Key to maps

●	Zone 1	below −50°F (−46°C)
●	Zone 2	−50° to −40°F (−46° to −40°C)
●	Zone 3	−40° to −30°F (−40° to −34.5°C)
●	Zone 4	−30° to −20°F (−34° to −29°C)
●	Zone 5	−20° to −10°F (−29° to −23°C)
●	Zone 6	−10° to 0°F (−23° to −18°C)
●	Zone 7	0° to 10°F (−18° to −12°C)
●	Zone 8	10° to 20°F (−12° to −7°C)
●	Zone 9	20° to 30°F (−7° to −1°C)
●	Zone 10	30° to 40°F (−1° to 4°C)
●	Zone 11	above 40°F (above 4°C)

Chapter 9

TOUGH CUSTOMERS

The rule we have adopted for this chapter is that the plants included within it should be able to fend for themselves – that is, once they are properly planted and established in their positions. Think of wild plants growing on a clifftop or on exposed moorland – these are some of the toughest plants Nature has come up with!

RIGHT *Grasses, as seen here at Windcliff Garden, Washington State, USA, are some of the toughest plants available for a coastal garden.*

What are tough plants?

Tough places to grow plants need tough plants to grow in them. This might sound blindingly obvious, but people often plant a delicate little thing in quite inhospitable conditions and are then surprised when it curls up its toes and dies.

Just what do we mean by 'tough'? Well, we are referring to any plant that, once planted in the right environment, can be expected to flourish with the minimum of cosseting and effort. Such a plant will be flexible, tenacious and able to endure hardship. Some plants are naturally hardier souls – what you might consider as the plant world equivalent of the 'street ruffian', able and willing to fight back.

However, not all of the plants featured in this chapter are tough in every respect. There may be some that endure gale-force winds with ease, but dislike intense cold. Others may be fine with a constant coastal battering, but they will not appreciate a wet soil.

A coastal garden, especially if it is also at altitude (such as on top of a cliff or hillside), can be one of the most inhospitable places for plants. When wind is combined with other conditions such as hail, extreme cold and, of course, salty air, its effect will be exacerbated.

Moorland areas, being of high altitude, will also be incredibly prone to strong winds, and low-growing moorland vegetation offers little defence; indeed it is the wind that ensures it remains close to the ground. Fortunately, there are some plants that willingly accept these sorts of conditions.

LEFT *Plants such as gorse* (Ulex europaeus) *can grow close to the sea and at high altitude because they are tough and durable.*

Brachyglottis 'Sunshine' AGM

Moorland plants

■ **Brachyglottis** (*Brachyglottis*)
This grey, felt-leaved, evergreen shrub is good for exposed, coastal places, as it tolerates salt spray. *Brachyglottis* 'Sunshine' AGM has yellow daisy flowers throughout summer and good foliage. *Brachyglottis monroi* AGM has a slightly denser habit. **USDA Zone:** Z8

■ **Butterfly bush** (*Buddleja davidii*)
This is a deciduous shrub, loved by butterflies and other nectar-loving insects. It does not mind wind or salt, and seems to thrive in cracks in paving and walls. Spikes of pink, purple or white blossoms appear amongst medium-green foliage. It can reach 15ft (4.5m), unless pruned. **USDA Zone:** Z5

■ **Gorse** (*Ulex europaeus*)
Gorse is a common shrub of lowland heath, with deep yellow flowers for much of the year. It survives on poor, impoverished soil and in full sun. It makes an effective and decorative barrier plant. Try the double-flowered 'Flore Pleno' AGM. **USDA Zone:** Z6

■ **Heather** (*Erica* spp and *Calluna* spp)
These are useful, tough plants, most of which require an acid soil in which to thrive. Winter-flowering types include forms of *Erica carnea* and *E.* x *darleyensis* (the taller-growing 'tree heathers'). For heathers flowering at other times, try: *E. vagans* (early summer to mid-autumn). **USDA Zone**: Z6–10

■ **Purple moor grass** (*Molinia caerulea*)
This grass comes from areas of damp, acidic moorland, but it is happy in most average to moist soils in sun or part shade. *Molinia caerulea* subsp *caerulea* 'Variegata' AGM makes attractive, tough little tussocks with yellowish stems. **USDA Zone:** Z5

■ **Wild rhododendron** (*Rhododendron ponticum*)
This plant is easy to grow in light shade and moisture-retentive, acidic or peaty soil. It has shallow roots, however, and so is not good for dry, sandy soil and desiccating winds. There are hundreds of forms, mostly spring-flowering. **USDA Zone:** Z5–9

Buddleja davidii 'Empire Blue' AGM

Ulex europaeus

Erica carnea 'King George'

Molinia caerulea subsp caerulea 'Variegata' AGM

Rhododendron ponticum

Hebe pinguifolia 'Pagei' AGM

Phalaris arundinacea

Tough garden plants

■ **Disc-leaved hebe** (*Hebe pinguifolia*)
This is a prostrate, evergreen shrub with tough, oval leaves making wide ground cover. It is decorated with small heads of pure white flowers for several weeks in late spring and early summer, for example, 'Pagei' AGM. It is much hardier than most of the taller *Hebe* hybrids. **USDA Zone:** Z6

■ **Elder** (*Sambucus nigra*)
Although this quick-growing shrub or tree can be pruned severely annually, it will reach 20ft (6m) in height. It is best in a mixed planting or as part of a hedgerow. Cream-white flowers appear in early summer, followed by black berries. The form 'Aurea' AGM has golden yellow leaves. **USDA Zone:** Z5

■ **Flowering currant** (*Ribes sanguineum*)
Ideal for a poor clay soil, this is a tough, deciduous shrub with clusters of pink flowers in spring. There are numerous named varieties. Look for 'Pulborough Scarlet' AGM (intense pink), 'King Edward VII' (slow growing and deep red) and 'Brocklebankii' AGM (pink flowers and golden foliage). **USDA Zone:** Z6

■ **Gardeners' garters** (*Phalaris arundinacea*)
Also known as reed canary grass and ribbon grass, this plant looks vibrant in silver, white and grey. If cut down when it looks slightly tired, it will produce a second crop of foliage for interest through the winter. 'Feesey's Form' – white leaves with narrow, green stripes – is arguably the best. **USDA Zone:** Z4

■ **Mexican daisy** (*Erigeron karvinskianus* AGM)
Originally from Mexico, this plant spreads across the ground and soon starts seeding itself into all sorts of odd spots. It has intricate, light green foliage and daisy flowers in long succession. **USDA Zone:** Z7

■ **Mountain ash, or rowan** (*Sorbus aucuparia*)
With a height of up to 50ft (15m) in some cultivars, this is not a tree for all gardens. But it is incredibly tough. Large, hanging clusters of orange-red fruits in autumn are the main feature. **USDA Zone:** Z2

Sambucus nigra 'Aurea' AGM

Erigeron karvinskianus AGM

Ribes sanguineum

Sorbus aucuparia

Phormium tenax 'Atropurpureum'

Cortaderia selloana

Kniphofia 'Royal Standard' AGM

■ New Zealand flax (*Phormium tenax*)

This evergreen perennial with arching, sword-shaped leaves makes a good focal point in a garden. Stout stems carry tight handfuls of dull red flowers. There are many varieties with green, yellow, cream, white, pink, red and purple leaves. One of the deepest forms is 'Atropurpureum'. **USDA Zone:** Z8

■ Pampas grass (*Cortaderia selloana*)

This plant is much used, often unwisely so, in small gardens. Clumps can reach 6ft (2m) across, with flower spikes reaching heights of 10ft (3m). Plants make a dense tussock of leaves topped by shaggy plumes in late summer and autumn. Well-drained soil in an open position is needed; examples are often found growing on the shoreline. **USDA Zone:** Z5

■ Red hot poker (*Kniphofia* spp)

These popular summer-flowering perennials are extremely windproof. They produce large rosettes of pointed leaves, although there are some diminutive forms with delicate, thin leaves. The poker-shaped flower heads are in shades of light yellow through to deep orange. **USDA Zone:** Z5–7

■ Sea holly (*Eryngium maritimum*)

There is nothing quite like the sea hollies, with their electric blue flowers. These thistle-like plants are hardy and cope well with wind. A well-grown specimen stands out in any border. Other excellent forms include *E. giganteum* AGM, *E. x tripartitum* AGM and *E. x oliverianum* AGM. **USDA Zone:** Z3–5

■ Spanish broom (*Spartium junceum* AGM)

This is considered 'weedy' by some gardeners, but it is a quick and easy small shrub that will help to fill gaps while slower, more prestigious shrubs are getting established. It has green stems and bright golden flowers, often coming in profusion. It withstands gales well. It prefers the sun and may be harmed in severely cold situations. **USDA Zone:** Z8

■ White-stemmed bramble

(*Rubus thibetanus* AGM)

This is a real toughie, but quite a dashing one. It is mainly grown for its winter stems, which glisten silvery white. The soft pink flowers are like small single roses, tucked in among the glossy, dark green foliage, which is white underneath. Black fruits appear in autumn. **USDA Zone:** Z6

Eryngium maritimum

Spartium junceum AGM

Rubus thibetanus AGM

Chapter 10

COASTAL TREES AND HEDGING

 If you are planting trees or shrubs specifically to reduce the wind speed as it hits your garden, you should try to choose subjects that are 'fit for purpose'. In other words, they should be happy growing in the most exposed of places. Garden hedging plants do not need to be quite so wind-tolerant, but they do have to be good wind filters, so the density of the branches and leaves becomes very important.

RIGHT *Trees form the perfect shelter belt, but they must be species that can cope with both wind and salty air conditions.*

Plants for windbreaks and hedges

This chapter covers which trees and shrubs are suitable for providing a windbreak and which are good for making formal and informal hedging and path edging.

Where a windbreak is concerned, the plants chosen – whether they are trees or large shrubs – will become effective only once they have reached a mature size. Therefore, do not expect the wind speed to be broken by small, young or underdeveloped plants.

In the biting wind near the cliff edge or along the shoreline, any rough vegetation will be welcome protection for a newly planted windbreak or hedge.

Native moorland plants (see page 117) as well as brambles, grasses and hardy bamboos, may be left on the windward side of the plants, if there is space for them. These plants will be tattered and singed by the wind, and are unlikely to reach their optimum height and decorative standard, but they are not there to be looked at – in fact, if they are on the seaward side of a windbreak, you may not get to see them at all.

There is not a great deal of choice when it comes to trees to form a shelter belt by the sea. The most effective are evergreen types, which will give protection all the year round, but there are also some very fine deciduous trees worth considering. These will be at their most efficient as wind filters when in full leaf, but in the winter they can still reduce wind speed on the leeward side significantly. Fortunately there is a much greater range of seaside shrubs that can be considered for use as windbreaks and hedges.

All of the plants included in this chapter will not mind being singed by salt spray. They will also tolerate high winds and, provided they are planted well and firmed and staked when young, should remain upright and firm at the roots.

LEFT *When planning windbreaks or hedges, look to see what is already growing well naturally.*

Nyssa sylvatica AGM

Trees for large gardens

■ **Black gum, or tupelo** (*Nyssa sylvatica* AGM)
This tree will grow up to 50ft (15m) in a sheltered position, but nearer 30ft (9m) in an exposed spot. Leathery, dark green leaves turn brilliant orange and red in autumn. It tolerates drought, but also grows well in wetlands. **USDA Zone:** Z3

■ **Chusan palm** (*Trachycarpus fortunei* AGM)
This evergreen palm has 3ft (90cm) wide, fan-shaped leaves, making it an ideal specimen tree for large lawns. It can reach 33ft (10m). Large heads of tiny, yellow flowers appear in late spring, sometimes followed by blue-black berries. **USDA Zone:** Z9

■ **Cider gum** (*Eucalyptus gunnii* AGM)
Most forms of *Eucalyptus* have attractive bark, handsome foliage and many-stamened white flowers. *E. gunnii* can reach 100ft (30m) or more, so in smaller gardens it is best coppiced, or grown as a multi-stemmed bush to 10ft (3m). **USDA Zone:** Z8

■ **False cypress** (*Chamaecyparis lawsoniana*)
This species of evergreen conifer has produced hundreds of forms, many of which are dwarf or slow-growing. The main species makes an excellent specimen tree with its narrow habit and dense foliage. It also makes a good, dense hedge, but can be clipped only into live foliage. **USDA Zone:** Z5–8

■ **Norway maple** (*Acer platanoides* AGM)
Most maples form large trees, or at least large shrubs. They make wonderful structural plantings, both for their foliage and bark. This form can reach as much as 80ft (24m), but usually nearer to 50ft (15m) if windswept. Salt-tolerant. **USDA Zone:** Z3

■ **Wattle** (*Acacia* spp)
Wattles like open sites in full sun and a well-drained soil, but not shallow chalk. They will die in extremely cold weather, but they do tolerate wind and salt well. *Acacia dealbata* AGM has silvery-green leaves and yellow flowers. **USDA Zone:** Z8

Trachycarpus fortunei AGM

Eucalyptus gunnii AGM

Chamaecyparis lawsoniana 'Stewartii'

Acer platanoides 'Drummondii'

Acacia dealbata AGM

Escallonia 'Apple Blossom' AGM

Elaeagnus pungens

Pittosporum tenuifolium AGM

Trees and shrubs for windbreaks

■ **Escallonia** (*Escallonia* spp)
These evergreen shrubs and small trees have pretty, small tubular flowers in pink, red or white. They withstand wind well, but are even better if given shelter. Excellent hybrids include 'Apple Blossom' AGM (pink and white flowers) and 'Donard Brilliance' (crimson). **USDA Zone:** Z7–9

■ **Oleaster** (*Elaeagnus pungens*)
The flowers of this evergreen shrub are not overtly decorative, but they are heavily fragrant. It is fast-growing and tolerant of wind. *Elaeagnus* x *ebbingei* is larger-growing – up to 5m. **USDA Zone:** Z2–10

■ **Pittosporum** (*Pittosporum tenuifolium* AGM)
In colder climates, some pittosporums can be damaged during hard winters, but they are excellent for coastal sites. *P. tenuifolium* is often seen, but *P. tobira* AGM is also common. **USDA Zone:** Z9

■ **Privet** (*Ligustrum* spp)
The privets can be either deciduous or evergreen shrubs and trees. *Ligustrum ovalifolium* is actually semi-evergreen, with mid-green leaves and clusters of tiny, white, fragrant flowers in mid summer. One of the best for a show of blooms is the deciduous *L. quihoui* AGM. **USDA Zone:** Z3–9

■ **Sea buckthorn** (*Hippophae rhamnoides* AGM)
This is an easy-going plant, thriving on sandy soil and in coastal gardens. It often fruits well, retaining its orange berries long after the silver, willow-like leaves have fallen. It is a useful plant where height is needed – it can grow to (or be kept to) anything between 3–30ft (1–9m). **USDA Zone:** Z3

■ **Tamarisk, or salt cedar** (*Tamarix ramosissima*)
These hardy, deciduous shrubs, native to Europe, Asia and Africa, are practically synonymous with seaside planting. Their pale to mid-green feather-like foliage looks delicate but can withstand heavy wind. Small rose-pink flowers are carried on spikes in late summer. The form 'Rubra' AGM has red flowers. **USDA Zone:** Z2

Ligustrum quihoui AGM

Hippophae rhamnoides AGM

Tamarix ramosissima

Formal hedges

Griselinia littoralis AGM

■ **Broadleaf** (*Griselinia littoralis* AGM)
This is an upright, fast-growing evergreen shrub or small tree of dense habit, grown for its apple-green leaves. These leaves are waxy-coated, making them resistant to wind and salt. Young growth can suffer in bitterly cold wind and frost. It grows best in full sun and a well-drained soil. **USDA Zone:** Z7

■ **Cherry laurel** (*Prunus laurocerasus* AGM)
This vigorous, wide-spreading evergreen shrub or small tree, if left untrimmed, can reach up to 20ft (6m). The leaves are leathery, glossy, green and oblong, and the flowers come in white heads in mid-spring, followed by purple-black fruits. **USDA Zone:** Z7

■ **Holly** (*Ilex* spp)
The common holly (*Ilex aquifolium* AGM) has numerous hybrids and cultivars. The species itself has dark green leaves and red berries. 'J.C. van Tol' AGM has narrow leaves with few spines and red berries; 'Golden King' has variegated leaves and red berries. **USDA Zone:** Z5–6

■ **Hornbeam** (*Carpinus betulus* AGM)
The common hornbeam is a graceful tree which can grow to more than 50ft (15m) high. In gardens it is best clipped as a hedge, where it makes an excellent wind filter. The green, ribbed and fluted leaves turn bright yellow in autumn. **USDA Zone:** Z5

■ **Sweet bay, or bay laurel** (*Laurus nobilis* AGM)
An aromatic, hardy, evergreen tree or shrub, from the Mediterranean, this plant usually forms a dense, pyramidal bush up to 20ft (6m). In mild, coastal regions it can be more tree-like. Small yellowish flowers appear in mid-spring. Bay is subject to browning in hard winters. **USDA Zone:** Z8

■ **Yew** (*Taxus baccata* AGM)
Yew will tolerate dry soil and reasonably dense shade, and can be clipped into a formal hedge. Go for the straight *Taxus baccata*, with mid- to deep green foliage and bright red berries. If left, it will make a large tree. All parts of the yew are poisonous. **USDA Zone:** Z6

Prunus laurocerasus AGM

Ilex aquifolium 'Golden King'

Carpinus betulus AGM

Laurus nobilis AGM

Taxus baccata AGM

Informal hedges

Pleioblastus variegatus 'Tsuboii'

Viburnum tinus

■ **Dwarf white-striped bamboo** (*Pleioblastus variegatus* AGM)
Most bamboos grow larger than this form, which reaches only 6ft (1.8m). It has broad leaves of apple green marked with wide cream bands. It can spread, but not excessively, and makes a fine hedge. 'Tsuboii' has the best colouring. **USDA Zone:** Z7

■ **Forest flame** (*Pieris formosa* var. *forrestii*)
This shrub is at its best in spring, when displays of white, bell-shaped blossoms appear, followed by young shoots in fiery reds or delicate pinks and creams. This new growth can be easily scorched by frost, so it is best suited to gardens where late frosts are rarer. *Pieris* need an acid soil. **USDA Zone:** Z5–7

■ **Hardy fuchsia** (*Fuchsia magellanica*)
Fuchsias are perhaps best known as pot plants or summer plants, but *F. magellanica* is a hardy form that can stay outside all year round. It may be harmed in a severely cold winter. Flowers are long, slender and red and purple. **USDA Zone:** Z6

Pieris formosa var. forrestii

Rosmarinus officinalis 'Miss Jessop's Upright' AGM

■ **Laurustinus** (*Viburnum tinus*)
A bushy, evergreen shrub, this durable plant has oval, mid-green leaves. White, pink-budded flowerheads are carried from late autumn through to late spring. Plants will grow to 6–10ft (1.8–3m) in height. 'Gwenllian' AGM and 'Eve Price' AGM are two excellent forms. **USDA Zone:** Z7

■ **Rosemary** (*Rosmarinus officinalis*)
Rosemary makes a fine aromatic plant in a sunny spot with a free-draining soil. It grows to around 5ft (1.5m) in height and has narrow grey-green leaves and clusters of small, pale blue flowers in spring and early summer. More upright in habit is 'Miss Jessop's Upright' AGM. **USDA Zone:** Z6–8

■ **Wild hedging rose** (*Rosa rugosa*)
Wild shrub roses are good for difficult seaside areas. *Rosa rugosa* flowers first in late spring on 6ft (2m) high canes, with deep, leathery foliage, then repeatedly throughout the summer. A very hardy species, it can tolerate salt spray, poor soil and drought. **USDA Zone:** Z2

Fuchsia magellanica

Rosa rugosa

Path edgings

Buxus sempervirens AGM

Lavandula stoechas AGM

■ **Box** (*Buxus sempervirens* AGM)
Box is perfect for training into low pathway hedging or even into topiary shapes. It is shade-tolerant, but variegated forms need full sun. **USDA Zone:** Z5

■ **Common myrtle** (*Myrtus communis* AGM)
The myrtle is an aromatic, evergreen shrub from warm regions. Against a sheltered, sunny wall it can reach a height and spread of 8–12ft (2.4–3.5m). White, fragrant flowers appear in summer, followed by black berries. Smaller, with finer leaves is M *communis* subsp. *tarentina* AGM. **USDA Zone:** Z8

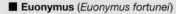

■ **Euonymus** (*Euonymus fortunei*)
This species of *Euonymus* may be trimmed to a shrub or left to grow into a small tree. The three most frequently seen forms are 'Emerald'n'Gold' AGM (with green, gold and pink leaves), 'Emerald Gaiety' AGM (green and cream leaves) and 'Silver Queen' (leaves with white edges). The waxy-coated leaves are good for repelling salt. **USDA Zone:** Z5

■ **Lavender** (*Lavandula* spp)
To many, lavender epitomizes dry soil and a sun-drenched climate. The old English lavender (*Lavandula angustifolia*) has pale blue flowers on long stems. There are many other excellent varieties, including 'Hidcote' AGM (violet flowers) and 'Hidcote Pink' (with pink flowers). The French lavender (*L. stoechas* AGM) has dark purple flowers topped by distinctive bracts. **USDA Zone:** Z5–9

■ **Skimmia** (*Skimmia* 'Rubella' AGM)
Skimmias are grown mostly for their rich, evergreen foliage and berries. Both male and female plants need to be grown to get the bright red berries. The flowering exception is 'Rubella' AGM, which has clusters of tiny, red flower buds. **USDA Zone:** Z7

■ **Spotted laurel** (*Aucuba japonica* 'Variegata')
This evergreen shrub grows in the most shaded and difficult of places. Rounded, evergreen leaves are richly coloured with cream and yellow spots. *Aucuba japonica* 'Picturata' has pointed leaves, whilst *A. japonica* 'Crotonifolia' AGM has more yellow in the leaves and produces berries freely. **USDA Zone:** Z7

Myrtus communis AGM

Skimmia 'Rubella' AGM

Euonymus fortunei 'Emerald'n'Gold' AGM

Aucuba japonica 'Variegata'

Chapter 11

COLOURFUL COASTAL PLANTS

For many people the challenge of producing an attractive garden by the sea is daunting enough, without worrying about whether it will still look good during the off seasons. Is it really possible to have a wonderfully colourful coastal windswept garden in the autumn and winter months? Absolutely!

RIGHT *Bright colours go hand-in-hand with the coastline and it is perfectly possible to create a vibrant coastal garden all year round.*

Colourful coastal plants season by season

So far in this book we have learned about the reasons why coastal gardens can be difficult, why wind and salt are problems and how to overcome them or compensate for them. We have also discovered that certain plants can be chosen to assist in reducing the problems of wind and salt; these plants provide shelter and can in effect change the climate and other dynamics of the garden.

Now, for the first time, we can begin to address the aesthetic qualities of the garden. From this point on, we can become rather more self-indulgent and concentrate on the plants that may be grown purely for their ornamental qualities.

Plants can be decorative in many ways. Most people – even non-gardeners – will think of flowers first as being the most attractive parts of plants. This is certainly true of some plants; however, there are several other features of plants that make them appealing to us – including stems, fruits and foliage. In this chapter we will be looking at everything except the foliage, which is studied in greater depth in Chapter 12.

In addition to the ornamental features of plants, it is important to consider when the plants are at their best. A garden that has a blaze of colour in one or two seasons, with nothing at all in the others, will be lacking any interest for at least half the year, so for this reason we have divided this chapter into the four seasons and suggested some decorative coastal plants for each.

LEFT *Pale blue harebells* (Campanula rolundifolia) *bedeck the chalk hills of the Isle of Purbeck, Dorset, UK.*

Celastrus orbiculatus

Winter colour

■ **Bittersweet** (*Celastrus orbiculatus*)
This is a climbing plant that provides wonderful winter colours from its berries. It reaches up to 46ft (14m) in height, its twining stems carrying handsome seeds, in green to golden pods. In the US, this plant carries a warning, as it has become troublesome in the wild. It is nevertheless an excellent plant for large gardens. **USDA Zone:** Z4

■ **Daphne** (*Daphne* spp)
The winter-flowering types include *Daphne odora* (evergreen) and *D. mezereum* (deciduous). Flowers are in various shades of pink, red or purple, and they give off an impressively powerful scent. **USDA Zone:** Z4–8

■ **Dogwood** (*Cornus* spp)
The *Cornus* is a huge family of trees and shrubs, but the species you need for winter colour are *C. alba* and *C. sericea*. Both are deciduous shrubs reaching around 7–10ft (2.5–3m). In the winter, after the leaves have dropped, the stems come alive with colour. Look for *C. alba* 'Sibirica' AGM and 'Spaethii' AGM (vivid red stems), and *C. sericea* 'Flaviramea' AGM (greenish yellow). **USDA Zone:** Z2–3

■ **Rhododendron** (*Rhododendron dauricum*)
There are several winter-flowering rhododendrons that are resilient enough to withstand some wind and salty air. *Rhododendron dauricum* is fully hardy and forms a small to medium-sized shrub. Its small trusses of flowers open from mid winter onwards. Look for 'Mid-Winter' AGM (clear mid-purple) and 'Olive' (crimson-blue). **USDA Zone:** Z5

■ **Silk tassel bush** (*Garrya elliptica*)
This vigorous, evergreen wall shrub has leathery leaves and conspicuous catkins from mid winter. The male plants have the best catkins; the female plants have purple-brown berries. **USDA Zone:** Z8

■ **Tree heath** (*Erica arborea*)
This can make a medium to large shrub, producing fragrant, creamy-white flowers at the end of winter. The variety 'Albert's Gold' AGM will eventually reach 6ft (2m); its upright branches bear bright golden-yellow foliage in winter. **USDA Zone:** Z7

Daphne odora

Cornus sericea 'Flaviramea' AGM

Rhododendron dauricum 'Olive'

Garrya elliptica

Erica arborea 'Albert's Gold' AGM

Rhododendron (Azalea) mollis

Cytisus 'La Coquette'

Ceanothus cuneatus var. rigidus

Spring colour

■ **Azalea** (*Rhododendron* spp)
Azaleas need an acid soil and part shade but do not mind wind and salty air. The deciduous types have riotous colour in late spring and early summer. *Azalea mollis* has bright yellow, highly scented blooms on almost leafless stems. **USDA Zone:** Z5–9

■ **Broom** (*Cytisus* spp)
The flowers of *Cytisus* come in such quantity that they clothe the whippy stems and tiny leaves. The pea-like flowers are in yellow, orange, cream and red shades, and there are several attractive bicolours, including 'La Coquette'. They tolerate poor, starved and sandy soils. **USDA Zone:** Z5–9

■ **Californian lilac** (*Ceanothus* spp)
One of the most attractive of all blue-flowering shrubs, this plant needs shelter and a sunny spot. The evergreen types such as *Ceanothus cuneatus* var. *rigidus* have small leaves and tight clusters of tiny flowers, while deciduous types have larger leaves and loose flower clusters. **USDA Zone:** Z4–8

■ **Camellia** (*Camellia* spp)
Camellias are woodland plants with glossy, green leaves. They like a moist, acid soil and part shade. They also appreciate a more sheltered garden, as both wind and frost can damage the blooms. The flowers come in colours from white through to pinks and reds. There are dozens of varieties, such as *Camellia* x *williamsii* 'Contribution'. **USDA Zone:** Z8

■ **Darwin's barberry** (*Berberis darwinii* AGM)
Berberis is a large genus of plants and most are tough and durable, so eminently suited to coastal gardens. For spring flower colour, try *B. darwinii*, an evergreen with small, dark green leaves and stunning displays of golden flowers. **USDA Zone:** Z7

■ **Flowering quince** (*Chaenomeles* spp)
Essential shrubs for late-winter interest, these plants look spectacular when trained against a wall. The flowers can be white, pink, red and orange; one of the best is *Chaenomeles* x *superba* 'Knap Hill Scarlet' AGM. They are tolerant of some shade, so are good for sunless walls. **USDA Zone:** Z5

Camellia x williamsii 'Contribution'

Berberis darwinii AGM

Chaenomeles x superba 'Knap Hill Scarlet' AGM

Forsythia x intermedia 'Spectabilis'

Kerria japonica 'Pleniflora' AGM

Syringa meyeri 'Palibin' AGM

■ **Golden bells** (*Forsythia* spp)
A ubiquitous plant, this has masses of flowers on the leafless branches. Colours range from pale yellows to deep golds. There are types to cover walls, grow as shrubs or hedges, or cover the ground. They are easy plants to grow; a good example is *Forsythia x intermedia* 'Spectabilis'. **USDA Zone:** Z5–6

■ **Jew's mallow** (*Kerria japonica*)
These spring-flowering, deciduous shrubs, bearing desirable yellow flowers, have a curious, upright, suckering habit. They do not object to a little shade, but they hate waterlogged soil. An attractive variety is 'Pleniflora' AGM, a double form with pompom-like flowers. **USDA Zone:** Z4

■ **Lilac** (*Syringa* spp)
There are dozens of lilac cultivars and most are forms of *Syringa vulgaris*, the common lilac. But there are many others; for example, *S. meyeri* 'Palibin' AGM. The flowering season for these plants is short, but the size and fragrance of the blooms more than make up for it. **USDA Zone:** Z4–6

■ **Magnolia** (*Magnolia stellata* AGM)
The tall tree magnolias are easily damaged by wind and salt, so in coastal gardens try the smaller, spring-flowering, shrubby types, such as the star magnolia. It is a good choice where space is limited, as it grows to just 4–5ft (1.2–1.5m). Early spring every year it is covered with fragrant, star-like flowers of creamy white. **USDA Zone:** Z4–9

■ **Mexican orange blossom** (*Choisya ternata* AGM)
This is a neat, rounded bush, well clothed with shiny, evergreen leaves that have a strong spicy fragrance when crushed. White, starry flowers appear as a main flush in mid- to late spring, then occasionally throughout the summer. It tolerates wind, salt and shade, and needs pruning only if it grows too big for its space. There is also a golden-leaved form. **USDA Zone:** Z7

■ **Weigela** (*Weigela florida*)
This very attractive and useful spring-flowering shrub has a reputation for succeeding in almost any garden and thriving despite blatant neglect. Tubular red or pink flowers are carried on arching stems in mid-spring. It does not grow very tall – 6–7ft (1.8–1.9m) at most. **USDA Zone:** Z5

Magnolia stellata AGM

Choisya ternata AGM

Weigela florida

Caryopteris x clandonensis

Callistemon rugulosus

Spiraea nipponica 'Snowmound' AGM

Summer colour

■ **Bluebeard, or blue spiraea** (*Caryopteris*)
Caryopteris is a small genus of mainly deciduous shrubs which has the double merit of being late-blooming and blue-flowered. The most often seen form is *Caryopteris* x *clandonensis* 'Arthur Simmonds' AGM, which reaches just 2ft (60cm) or so, and has bright blue flowers. The variety 'Kew Blue' is a deeper shade. **USDA Zone:** Z6–8

■ **Bottlebrush** (*Callistemon*)
Native to Australia, the evergreen bottlebrushes, such as *Callistemon rugulosus*, bring a quirky, exotic touch to the coastal garden. They produce vivid, brush-like flowers. They are not the hardiest of shrubs and really only thrive in fairly mild climates or protected, sheltered gardens. **USDA Zone:** Z9

■ **Bridal wreath** (*Spiraea* spp)
This is a popular group of quick-growing shrubs, which are easy to grow and always flower. Tiny, pink or white flowers are massed in clusters on arching stems. *Spiraea nipponica* 'Snowmound' AGM is an outstanding form for early summer. It tolerates hard pruning and can be kept smaller than its usual height of 6ft (2m). **USDA Zone:** Z4

■ **Cape figwort** (*Phygelius capensis* AGM)
Phygelius is a sub-shrub. It is evergreen in a mild winter, but may die back in prolonged cold, although it will often reshoot. In a cold or exposed garden, grow in the lee of a wall. **USDA Zone:** Z8

■ **Common hydrangea** (*Hydrangea macrophylla*)
The Japanese species is rarely seen in cultivation, but it is widely represented by many selected forms. They are divided mainly into mophead and lacecap types and they have blue, pink or white flowerheads. Give them a little shade and do not let them dry out. Otherwise they are easy plants. **USDA Zone:** Z5

■ **Deutzia** (*Deutzia* spp)
The elegant, deciduous deutzias are grown for their dainty, early summer flowers. Perfect for a coastal cottage garden, they will usually succeed in any soil, in full sun or light shade. One of the most attractive is *Deutzia scabra* 'Plena', with small double flowers of white, flushed purplish pink. **USDA Zone:** Z4–8

Phygelius x rectus 'Winchester Fanfare'

Hydrangea macrophylla

Deutzia scabra 'Plena'

Abutilon x hybridum

x Halimiocistus wintonensis 'Merrist Wood Cream' AGM

Phlomis fruticosa AGM

■ **Flowering, or Indian mallow** (*Abutilon* spp)
These elegant, tender shrubs produce appealing lampshade-like flowers during late summer. They are sometimes trained as standards, or grown as tall 'accent' plants to separate a carpet of bedding plants. They also make fine plants for containers. There are many hybrids available in yellows, orange and pinks. **USDA Zone:** Z8–10

■ **Halimiocistus** (x *Halimiocistus wintonensis* AGM)
This is an evergreen shrub, which is a cross between the genera *Halimium* and *Cistus*, both of which hybridize naturally in the wild. It has papery flowers that are saucer shaped and likes a sunny spot in a free draining soil. The cultivar 'Merrist Wood Cream' AGM, has cream flowers marked with yellow and maroon. **USDA Zone:** Z8

■ **Jerusalem sage** (*Phlomis fruticosa* AGM)
These evergreen shrubs and perennials have woolly grey leaves. Whorls of sulphur-yellow flowers appear in summer. They are well suited to a Mediterranean-style border and grown with such plants as *Cistus* or *Halimium*. **USDA Zone:** Z7–9

■ **Lavender cotton** (*Santolina* spp)
This is a mound-forming shrub with finely dissected, silvery leaves. It has lemon-yellow flowers in mid summer, but it is principally valued as a foliage plant. Take a pair of shears to it in spring to neaten it, if necessary, but old, straggly plants are best replaced. **USDA Zone:** Z7

■ **Lobster's claw, or parrot's bill** (*Clianthus puniceus* AGM)
This is an exotic member of the pea family from New Zealand. It is semi-evergreen and strong-growing, but will thrive outside only in mild gardens. It has a sprawling habit and its leaves have many leaflets, rather like vetch. The early summer flowers are red and claw-like with black eyes. **USDA Zone:** Z8

■ **Mock orange blossom** (*Philadelphus* spp)
The scent of this plant is unmistakable when it hangs in the air in early summer. Most of the plants in cultivation are hybrids, have white flowers with golden stamens and are best when grown as a fragrant backdrop to a mixed border. These plants do well in most reasonable soils and in full sun or light shade. **USDA Zone:** Z5–9

Santolina chamaecyparissus AGM

Clianthus puniceus AGM

Philadelphus 'Belle Etoile' AGM

Hoheria lyallii AGM

Cistus x purpureus AGM

Rosa 'Penelope' (Floribunda)

■ **Ribbonwood** (*Hoheria lyallii* AGM)
These are garden trees from New Zealand and, although they tolerate salty air, they are not for cold or exposed gardens. The two most common species are *Hoheria sexstylosa* and *H. lyallii* AGM. The first is an evergreen; the second is deciduous. Both have a light, airy habit and showers of starry, white flowers in the summer. **USDA Zone:** Z8

■ **Rock, or sun rose** (*Cistus* x *purpureus* AGM)
In Mediterranean countries, these evergreen shrubs are seen everywhere. The flowers have a papery texture, like poppies, and are short-lived. However, they follow one another in quick succession at the height of summer. They are perfect in scree, gravel or sandy gardens, basking in the reflected heat from the ground. **USDA Zone:** Z7–8

■ **Roses** (*Rosa* spp)
As a garden plant, roses are unrivalled. Hybrid teas and floribundas such as the floribunda bush rose 'Penelope' make a good choice for windy, salt-swept gardens, mainly because the new growth lasts for only one growing year, before it is cut down. The more shelter you can provide, though, the longer the blowsy blooms will last. **USDA Zone:** Z5–7

■ **St John's wort** (*Hypericum* spp)
These shrubs can sometimes be awkward to place in a garden because of the uncompromising yellow of the flowers. They do look good, though, with white-flowered or purple-leaved plants. Grow them in any well-drained soil in full sun or light shade. **USDA Zone:** Z6

■ **Shrubby cinquefoil** (*Potentilla fruticosa*)
There are many forms of this low-growing shrub and they all bear masses of small, rose-like flowers in summer. It is a good choice for the front of a border, along a path or even on a rock garden. *Potentilla* grows in most well-drained soils in sun or light shade. **USDA Zone:** Z2–8

■ **Tree mallow** (*Lavatera x clementii* 'Rosea' AGM)
A genus of evergreen, semi-evergreen and deciduous shrubs, the shrubby form is prized for its late summer blooms. It reaches 3–4ft (1–1.2m) in height, is bushy and upright, with green, lobed leaves and purplish-pink flowers. 'Rosea' AGM has flowers of a brighter pink. **USDA Zone:** Z8–9

Hypericum calycinum

Potentilla recta 'Warrenii'

Lavatera x clementii 'Rosea' AGM

Autumn colour

■ Eupatorium (*Eupatorium* spp)
The *Eupatorium* genus comprises perennial plants with long-lasting, broad, purple, pink and white flowerheads, usually from late summer. Plants can frequently grow taller than 6ft (2m) in a season and look good at the back of a border. **USDA Zone:** Z3–7

■ Firethorn (*Pyracantha* spp)
These evergreen shrubs have spiny branches, bright, small summer flowers and prolific autumn berries. They make fine wall and hedging plants. Two worth mentioning are *Pyracantha* 'Navaho' with vivid orange berries and *P. rogersiana* 'Flava' AGM with bright yellow berries. **USDA Zone:** Z6–8

■ Hardy plumbago
(*Ceratostigma plumbaginoides* AGM)
This is a somewhat tender (despite its common name) perennial or sub-shrub, with bristly, many-branched, reddish stems and purplish-blue flowers throughout autumn. Plants grow to a height of just 12–18in (30–45cm). This plant can be invasive over time – but is easily controlled. **USDA Zone:** Z5

■ Herringbone cotoneaster
(*Cotoneaster horizontalis* AGM)
The *Cotoneaster* genus is huge and all are tough, durable plants. The herringbone cotoneaster will reach just 2–3ft (60–100cm) if grown prostrate, whereas against a wall it can grow to 10ft (3m). Tiny spring flowers are followed by profuse bright red berries in autumn. **USDA Zone:** Z4

■ Shrubby veronica (*Hebe* spp)
There are many different forms of these pretty shrubs with oval or pointed leaves and spikes of flowers. Try 'Autumn Glory' (deep purple-blue spikes) and 'Marjorie' (one of the hardiest, with light violet flowers). **USDA Zone:** Z6–9

■ Snowberry (*Symphoricarpos* spp)
This is a deciduous shrub which is grown mainly for its autumn berries. The forms most often seen are *Symphoricarpos albus*, with glistening white berries, and *S.* x *doorenbosii*, with slightly smaller fruits. Forms of this include 'White Hedge' and 'Mother of Pearl'. **USDA Zone:** Z3–4

Eupatorium hybrid

Pyracantha 'Navaho'

Ceratostigma plumbaginoides AGM

Cotoneaster horizontalis AGM

Hebe 'Marjorie'

Symphoricarpos x doorenbosii 'White Hedge'

Chapter 12

STUNNING FOLIAGE FOR COLOUR

Plants with attractive leaves, whether they are silver, gold, red or yellow, are good 'rent payers'. This means that they give a good account of themselves for several months of the year, unlike those grown just for their flowers, which may last just a week or two – or less.

RIGHT *Foliage form and colour provided by cordylines, agaves and a variety of other succulents at the gardens of Tresco, Cornwall, UK.*

Stunning foliage plants for colour

Many gardeners select plants because of their flowers or fruits, or to a lesser extent bark. The foliage is often not considered as a decorative feature. But there are plenty of plants that are grown for their leaves rather than anything else. All of the plants chosen in this chapter are well suited to coastal gardens and have been segregated into four different colour groups.

First there are the silver-, grey- and blue-leaved plants, which are amongst the most useful and beautiful of all garden plants. They serve as accent plants to enhance stronger-coloured plants around them, and most are evergreens, so even on the bleakest of winter days they shine like beacons in dull, lifeless borders. Silver leaves are actually green leaves covered with a mass of fine, silky hairs, which protect the leaves of plants living in arid areas from intense sun and drying winds. This makes them, in general, excellent coastal plants.

Then there are plants with gold and yellow leaves, many of which are evergreens. They are popular and familiar plants as they are often chosen by municipal landscapers for their year-round appeal and ease of maintenance. As with the silver plants, the evergreen forms will add a touch of sunshine to a winter garden.

Red-, purple- and plum-leaved plants form another group. These plants can transform a border with their warm colour tones. More of these are deciduous by nature, so in the autumn the maroon and plum tones often turn to fiery reds and orange.

Then, finally, are the variegated plants. In most cases these have been bred from normal green-leaved species, to give more interest in the border. The leaves can be beautiful in their own right, and the plants with proportionately more creams or yellows in the leaves can be stunning.

LEFT At Abbotsbury Subtropical Gardens, Dorset, UK, banana plants provide height, while lower plants give form and colour.

Silver, blue and grey foliage

Arctotis x hybrida 'Wine'

Meum amathanticum

Festuca glauca 'Blaufuchs' AGM

■ **Arctotis** (*Arctotis* x *hybrida*)
This South African genus is well known for its orange daisy flowers from the annual species *Arctotis fastuosa*. But it also has a perennial species, and a good one for coastal gardens is the silver-leaved *A.* x *hybrida* and its cultivars, which includes 'Wine' with pale, reddish-purple flowers. **USDA Zone:** Z9

■ **Baldmoney, or spignel** (*Meum amathanticum*)
This is a perennial, thistle-like plant grown for its attractive, aromatic leaves. Thistle-like flowerheads, in white or purplish white, appear in summer. It is fully hardy, but needs a well-drained soil and a position in full sun. **USDA Zone:** Z7

■ **Blue fescue** (*Festuca glauca*)
Festuca glauca 'Blaufuchs' AGM (or 'Blue Fox') is one of the best blue-leaved grasses. It reaches just 6in (15cm) in height and is perfect in containers or the front of a border. **USDA Zone:** Z5

■ **Butterfly bush** (*Buddleja* spp)
Many buddleias have a silvery sheen to the stems and leaves, which is probably best exemplified in the hybrid 'Lochinch' AGM. The leaves are grey-green, white beneath, and the late summer flowers are mauve, with an orange centre. **USDA Zone:** Z5

■ **Cardoon** (*Cynara cardunculus* AGM)
This stately, thistle-like plant is a deciduous perennial. Large, violet-blue thistle flowers appear in summer and early autumn, but the large leaves are the main feature, offering structure to a border. **USDA Zone:** Z6

■ **Colorado blue spruce** (*Picea pungens*)
This conifer can reach 100ft (30m) in the wild, but its garden cultivars are closer to 10ft (3m) after 10 years or so. Mostly grey-green, with sharply pointed prickly leaves, its new growth each spring is bluer and softer. It also has light brown winter buds. Give it a position in full sun. The form 'Blue Mountain' has more intense blue colouring. **USDA Zone:** Z2–8

Buddleja 'Lochinch' AGM

Cynara cardunculus AGM

Picea pungens 'Blue Mountain'

Lamium galeobdolon 'Hermann's Pride'

Euryops pectinatus AGM

Stachys byzantina

■ **Dead-nettle** (*Lamium galeobdolon*)
This perennial is generally grown as a ground cover plant. It spreads by creeping stems, and its most commonly seen form is 'Variegatum' with pink flowers and leaves marbled silver-grey. Even better is the form 'Hermann's Pride', with mainly silver leaves and green veining. **USDA Zone:** Z6

■ **Euryops** (*Euryops pectinatus* AGM)
The grey-green foliage of this shrubby perennial is very attractive. Up to 4in (10cm), the leaves are deeply lobed, with very narrow individual segments (the Latin *pectinatus* means comb-like). In summer, the solitary, buttercup-yellow daisy flowers appear. It is an excellent container and patio plant. **USDA Zone:** Z8

■ **Lamb's ears** (*Stachys byzantina*)
This must be one of the best-loved of silver plants. The best time for it is late spring, when the fur covering the leaves is at its most dense. The flowers, which come in upright spikes in mid summer, are of secondary value, which is why the flowerless form 'Silver Carpet' is so popular. **USDA Zone:** Z5

■ **Lawson cypress** (*Chamaecyparis lawsoniana*)
The straight species has given rise to a multitude of cultivars, many of which are in the 40 shades of green. One or two are notably blue/silver – arguably the best is 'Chilworth Silver' AGM. Look out also for 'Bleu Nantais' and 'Blue Surprise'. These all grow to a height of 5ft (1.5m) or so. **USDA Zone:** Z6–8

■ **Penstemon** (*Penstemon hirsutus* var. *pygmaeus*)
This popular genus of perennials is not generally known for its silver foliage. However, there is one form, which makes an excellent low plant for the front of a border: *Penstemon hirsutus* var. *pygmaeus*. The *hirsutus* is Latin for 'hairy' and *pygmaeus* means 'small'. The plant reaches just 6in (15cm) or so, and produces violet flowers in summer. **USDA Zone:** Z3

■ **Rue** (*Ruta graveolens*)
This herb, with its deeply divided, grey-green leaves, which are almost evergreen, looks good in beds and containers. But the strong coconut smell of the foliage is disliked by some. It reaches a height of 2–3ft (60–90cm). The variety 'Jackman's Blue' has leaves of a stronger blue-grey. **USDA Zone:** Z5

Chamaecyparis lawsoniana 'Chilworth Silver' AGM

Penstemon hirsutus var. pygmaeus

Ruta graveolens

Perovskia 'Blue Haze'

Crambe maritima AGM

Convolvulus cneorum AGM

■ **Russian sage** (*Perovskia atriplicifolia*)
With silver, mint-scented foliage and tiny blue-purple flowers growing along stalks, rather like lavender, this low shrub is a sun-lover. It is even better on a chalky soil. The hybrid 'Blue Haze' has lavender-purple flowers, whilst 'Blue Spire' AGM is a deeper violet-blue. **USDA Zone:** Z6

■ **Seakale** (*Crambe maritima* AGM)
The common name of this easy-to-grow perennial indicates its ability to grow in sandy soil, near the sea. It also likes full sun. It has a central crown surrounded by a mound of large, textured, blue-grey leaves. In summer, the plants are also covered with small white flowers. **USDA Zone:** Z5

■ **Shrubby convolvulus** (*Convolvulus cneorum* AGM)
This evergreen, silver-leaved shrub reaches a height of 2–3ft (60–90cm). Small, white and very pale pink trumpet flowers appear throughout summer. It is not completely hardy and can be cut back in cold winters. It will thrive in a spot protected by a sunny wall. **USDA Zone:** Z8

■ **Silver thistle** (*Onopordum acanthium*)
This, it is said, was the original thistle brought back from the Holy Land by the Crusaders, and which was adopted as the emblem of Scotland. It looks magnificent at the back of a summer border; it grows to about 5ft (1.5m), so will usually be seen towering over shorter plants further forward. The leaves are silvery and the stems nearly white. **USDA Zone:** Z6

■ **Trailing helichrysum**
(*Helichrysum petiolare* AGM)
This plant, with silver, heart-shaped leaves ½in (1cm) across, appears white rather than silver, and its main charm is in the arching habit of the branches, which always curve towards the ground. It is probably best in a container, as it trails nicely. **USDA Zone:** Z10

■ **Wormwood** (*Artemisia arborescens* AGM)
This shrub, which is arguably the most beautiful of all the silvers, needs good drainage and a light, sandy soil. In summer, the silky foliage has a silvery sheen. The flowering stems, generally few and far between, have no decorative value and should be cut off. 'Faith Raven' has very finely cut leaves. **USDA Zone:** Z8

Onopordum acanthium

Helichrysum petiolare AGM

Artemisia arborescens 'Faith Raven'

Milium effusum 'Aureum' AGM

Sambucus nigra 'Aurea' AGM

Yellow and gold foliage

■ **Bowles' golden grass** (*Milium effusum*)
This perennial grass reaches just 12in (30cm) or so in height, with a similar spread. In the straight species (wood millet), clumps of soft-green, grassy leaves are produced, but in the form 'Aureum' AGM, they are bright yellow. **USDA Zone:** Z6

■ **Escallonia** (*Escallonia laevis* 'Gold Ellen')
These shrubs make good windbreaks. In the form 'Gold Ellen', the bright yellow leaves are the main feature and the pink flowers are somewhat surplus to requirements. **USDA Zone:** Z7–9

■ **Golden caryopteris** (*Caryopteris* x *clandonensis* 'Worcester Gold' AGM)
Caryopteris is both late-blooming and blue-flowered (see page 134). In this form it is also golden-leaved. It reaches a height of 5ft (1.5m) and is a good plant for a windy, sunny spot by the sea. **USDA Zone:** Z7

■ **Golden elder** (*Sambucus nigra* 'Aurea' AGM)
This shrub can reach 10ft (3m), but it responds well to pruning to keep it small. The leaves usually have five leaflets and are golden yellow (mid-green in the straight species). Fragrant cream-white flowers, with flattened heads, appear in early summer, followed by black fruits in autumn. **USDA Zone:** Z5

■ **Golden juniper** (*Juniperus* x *pfitzeriana* 'Gold Star')
This low, prostrate, flattish conifer, bred in Canada, has almost wholly juvenile foliage. It is bright, golden yellow in summer and much more green-gold in winter. Look out also for 'Gold Coast', 'Carbery Gold' and 'Golden Saucer'. **USDA Zone:** Z3

■ **Golden marjoram** (*Origanum vulgare*)
This is a tender perennial, but is best grown fresh every year, as an annual. The normal species has greyish-green, slightly hairy leaves and small, round heads of cream-white flowers. The golden-leaved form 'Aureum' AGM is much more ornamental.
USDA Zone: Z10–11

Escallonia laevis 'Gold Ellen'

Juniperus x pfitzeriana 'Gold Star'

Caryopteris x clandonensis 'Worcester Gold' AGM

Origanum vulgare 'Aureum' AGM

Philadelphus coronarius 'Aureus' AGM

Ligustrum ovalifolium 'Aureum' AGM

Lonicera nitida 'Baggeson's Gold' AGM

■ **Golden mock orange** (*Philadelphus coronarius* 'Aureus' AGM)
Unlike many golden-leaved plants, this form of mock orange does well in shade; here the leaves remain fresh, whereas in full sun they can scorch. It is more compact than most other *Philadelphus*. The leaves turn greener as they age. **USDA Zone:** Z5

■ **Golden privet** (*Ligustrum ovalifolium* 'Aureum' AGM)
Some of the best coastal hedges comprise the golden privet, or the golden and plain green privet alternately planted. This semi-evergreen species has leaves that are golden yellow at the margins and a pale green-yellow in the centres. Tiny, white, fragrant flowers appear in summer. **USDA Zone:** Z5

■ **Golden small-leaved lonicera** (*Lonicera nitida*)
The straight species makes a good low hedge. Its green leaves are small and the branches become quite dense, making a good barrier. It can grow to 10ft (3m) in height, but is best kept to around 3ft (1m). 'Baggeson's Gold' AGM is a slow-growing, golden-leaved variety. **USDA Zone:** Z7

■ **Hardy fuchsia** (*Fuchsia magellanica* var *gracilis* 'Aurea' AGM)
With bright yellow leaves, this hardy fuchsia will reach a height of 4ft (1.2m), but can be cut back almost to ground level at the end of winter. The flowers are red and red-violet. It is not such a hardy plant as the green-leaved parent, but it is still worth trying in a mild, coastal location. **USDA Zone:** Z6

■ **Lawson cypress** (*Chamaecyparis lawsoniana* 'Ellwood's Gold' AGM)
This was the first form of Lawson cypress with golden foliage, but the colour is pronounced only in summer on new growth and is more evident on younger plants. In winter the foliage is decidedly green. After 10 years this conifer reaches 5–6ft (1.5–1.8m). **USDA Zone:** Z6–8

■ **Shrubby veronica** (*Hebe ochracea* 'James Stirling' AGM)
This is one of the so-called 'whipcord' *Hebes*, where the leaves are held tight to the stems and are rather scale-like. It has deep golden foliage and white flowers in summer. It reaches 18in (45cm) in height and can be short-lived. **USDA Zone:** Z6

Fuchsia magellanica var gracilis 'Aurea' AGM

Chamaecyparis lawsoniana 'Ellwood's Gold' AGM

Hebe ochracea 'James Stirling' AGM

Epimedium x versicolor 'Sulphureum' AGM

Red, purple and plum foliage

■ **Barrenwort** (*Epimedium* x *versicolor* 'Sulphureum' AGM)
This evergreen perennial, originally from North Africa, makes a good ground cover plant. It is grown for its leaves, which turn, through the season, to various shades of red. The pale yellow flowers give rise to the cultivar name. **USDA Zone:** Z5

■ **Shrubby veronica** (*Hebe* 'Caledonia')
Unlike the whipcord hebes (p145), this is one of the large-leaved types, which has maroon-green leaves and violet-blue flowers, each with a white eye.
USDA Zone: Z8

■ **Castor oil plant** (*Ricinus communis*)
This annual has attractive summer foliage and makes a good accent plant with low-growing bedding plants. Its leaves are large with maroon or bronze tints. 'Carmencita' AGM has dark brown foliage and 'Impala' is bronze-maroon when young. The seeds are poisonous. **USDA Zone:** Z9

■ **Eastern redbud** (*Cercis canadensis* 'Forest Pansy' AGM)
A deciduous, spreading shrub or small tree, it can reach a height of 30ft (10m) if left to its own devices. It has heart-shaped, reddish-purple leaves. In mid-spring, small, whitish flowers (that are pink in bud) are carried in profusion. **USDA Zone:** Z4

■ **New Zealand flax** (*Phormium tenax*)
We have already seen that phormiums are incredibly tough plants (p119). There are several that are grown for their red or purple leaves, including 'Bronze Baby', Amazing Red' and 'Black Edge'. *Phormium* 'Platt's Black' is useful in contemporary planting schemes. **USDA Zone:** Z8

■ **Purple elder** (*Sambucus nigra* f. *porphyrophylla* 'Black Beauty' or 'Gerda' AGM)
Similar to 'Aurea' (p144) this shrub can reach 10ft (3m) or so, but can be pruned. The lobed leaves are blackish purple. **USDA Zone:** Z5

Cercis canadensis 'Forest Pansy' AGM

Phormium 'Platt's Black'

Hebe 'Caledonia'

Ricinus communis

Sambucus nigra f. porphyrophylla 'Black Beauty' AGM

Photinia fraseri 'Red Robin' AGM

Euphorbia x martini 'Helena's Blush'

Physocarpus opulifolius 'Diabolo' AGM

■ **Photinia** (*Photinia fraseri* 'Red Robin' AGM)
This is one of the most frequently planted shrubs for parks and public spaces. It is easy to maintain and is a real spectacle in spring when its new growth emerges as bright red, glossy leaves. As these mature they turn green, and being evergreen will last for several years. It can reach a height of 20ft (6m), but can be easily trimmed. **USDA Zone:** Z8

■ **Red-leaved spurge** (*Euphorbia* x *martini* 'Helena's Blush')
This hybrid has petite green-and-cream variegated foliage with a hint of pink on the undersides. It produces chartreuse and apple-green bicoloured bracts on airy stems. It prefers partial shade and moist but well-drained soil. Its milky sap can cause skin irritation and pain if ingested. **USDA Zone:** Z7

■ **Red ninebark** (*Physocarpus opulifolius*)
This is an underrated genus of deciduous shrubs, distantly related to the rose. Arching branches are clothed in oval, toothed leaves; these are mid-green in the straight species, but deep plum in 'Diabolo'. Clusters of tiny, white, sometimes pink-tinged, flowers appear in early summer. **USDA Zone:** Z2

■ **Red sage** (*Salvia officinalis* 'Purpurascens' AGM)
Sage is a wonderfully fragrant garden plant. The red sage (actually more bronze-green) is a handsome variety with leaves that are even stronger in flavour than the green form. Plants grow to a height of 24–32in (60–80cm). **USDA Zone:** Z5

■ **Cabbage palm** (*Cordyline australis*)
The plain green form makes a slow-growing bushy tree. Sword-shaped leaves up to 3ft (90cm) long are borne in large clusters, either centrally in a rosette (in young plants) or at the end of stiff branches (in older plants). Cream-white fragrant flowers in loose, branched heads appear in early summer. There are a number of reddish-leaved cultivars and 'Torbay Red' AGM is one of the best. **USDA Zone:** Z10

■ **Smoke tree** (*Cotinus coggygria* 'Royal Purple' AGM)
This cultivar of the popular smoke tree has deep wine-purple leaves all season; in this respect it is very similar to 'Notcutt's Variety'. Plants have a filmy, pinkish grey inflorescence partly covered in silky hairs in mid summer. **USDA Zone:** Z5

Salvia officinalis 'Purpurascens' AGM

Cordyline australis 'Torbay Red' AGM

Cotinus coggygria 'Royal Purple' AGM

Hedera helix 'Oro di Bogliasco'

Variegated foliage

■ **Goldheart ivy** (*Hedera helix* 'Oro di Bogliasco')
Hedera helix is the common ivy. Although to many people it is a pest, there are some very fine variegated forms. The best is probably 'Oro di Bogliasco'. **USDA Zone:** Z5

■ **Luma** (*Luma apiculata* 'Glanleam Gold' AGM)
This is a strong-growing, upright, evergreen shrub, reaching 30ft (10m) when mature. However, it can be clipped to keep it small. It has sturdy stems with peeling brown and white bark. The leaves are bright green with cream-yellow edges. **USDA Zone:** Z9

■ **Shrubby veronica** (*Hebe* x *andersonii* 'Andersonii Variegata')
Unlike the whipcord hebes (p145), this is a large-leaved type, and has probably the strongest variegation of any hebe. It has violet flowers in summer. **USDA Zone:** Z9

■ **Silver hedgehog holly** (*Ilex aquifolium* 'Ferox Argentea' AGM)
Ilex aquifolium is the common holly, and there are dozens of varieties – all are excellent for coastal gardens. One of the most intriguing is the silver hedgehog holly which, like its green counterpart, has spines all over the leaf surface. **USDA Zone:** Z6

■ **Variegated century plant** (*Agave americana* 'Variegata' AGM)
The *Agave* is a spiky, architectural plant, but is frost-tender, so keep in a pot and move to a greenhouse for the winter. The variegated form has a central grey-green band. **USDA Zone:** Z9

■ **Variegated false castor oil plant** (*Fatsia japonica* 'Variegata' AGM)
The plain green *Fatsia* is big, glossy, evergreen and quite hardy. It is better in dappled to dense shade and under the protection of a wall. 'Variegata' has a very subtle variegation: the grey-green leaves are tipped with creamy white. **USDA Zone:** Z8

Ilex aquifolium 'Ferox Argentea' AGM

Luma apiculata 'Glanleam Gold' AGM

Agave americana 'Variegata' AGM

Hebe x andersonii 'Andersonii Variegata'

Fatsia japonica 'Variegata' AGM

Fuchsia 'John Ridding'

Polemonium caeruleum 'Brise d'Anjou'

Pieris japonica 'Carnaval'

■ **Variegated fuchsia** (*Fuchsia* 'John Ridding')
This lovely variegated fuchsia may be sold under this name or 'Firecracker'. It is an upright deciduous shrub with an arching habit. Its leaves are grey-green and cream variegated, flushed pink and with pink undersides. It is frost-tender, so should be overwintered under cover. **USDA Zone:** Z9

■ **Variegated Jacob's ladder** (*Polemonium caeruleum* 'Brise d'Anjou')
Just like its green counterpart, the plant makes a hummock and the foliage is set like the rungs of a ladder along the stalks. Blue or white flowers appear in early summer, but the silver-green and white foliage of this plant is outstanding. **USDA Zone:** Z2

■ **Variegated lily of the valley bush** (*Pieris japonica* 'Carnaval')
Straight *Pieris japonica* has a height and spread of some 6–10ft (1.8–3m) and, being a relative of the *Rhododendron*, is best in a semi-shaded situation and in an acid or peaty soil. There are several variegated forms; one of the best is 'Carnaval', with white margins and pink flushes. **USDA Zone:** Z6

■ **Variegated oleaster** (*Elaeagnus* spp)
As we saw on p124, these are tough plants suitable for windbreaks, hedges and shelter belts. The variegated forms brighten a winter garden with their bright yellow blotches, patches and splodges. Four of the best are *E.* x *ebbingei* 'Coastal Gold', 'Gilt Edge' AGM, 'Gold Splash' and *E. pungens* 'Goldrim' AGM. **USDA Zone:** Z2–10

■ **Variegated Chinese olive** (*Osmanthus heterophyllus* 'Variegatus' AGM)
This is a slow-growing, evergreen shrub with holly-shaped leaves that have half-green and half-cream blotches. The shrub will reach a height and spread of 6–8ft (1.8–2.4m), and it produces tubular flower clusters in early autumn. **USDA Zone:** Z6

■ **Variegated pittosporum** (*Pittosporum eugenioides* 'Variegatum' AGM)
All pittosporums are good subjects for the coastal garden. This is a columnar, evergreen tree that will possibly reach 30ft (10m) or so when mature. Narrowly oval, wavy-edged leaves are glossy, dark green with a narrow white margin. **USDA Zone:** Z9

Elaeagnus pungens 'Goldrim' AGM

Osmanthus heterophyllus 'Variegatus' AGM

Pittosporum eugenioides 'Variegatum' AGM

Chapter 13

ANNUALS AND BEDDING PLANTS FOR COLOUR

 Anyone who has visited a seaside town will probably remember seeing large beds of brightly coloured flowers along the promenades. These beds are filled mainly with annual plants, some of the brightest, most vividly coloured plants available – and they can be grown with just as much success and impact in our own coastal gardens.

RIGHT *Annuals – including red poppies, white nicotiana and other meadow flowers – abound in this coastal garden.*

Coastal colour from annuals and bedding plants

'**Bedding plants' is a term that gardeners do not always fully understand. Most bedding plants are annuals. These are plants that are sown, grow, flower and die all within a year. Bedding plants can also be biennials, which are sown and grown on in one year, and flower and die during a second year.**

Confusingly, however, there are a number of perennial plants, and even soft shrubs, that are grown as bedding plants nowadays. It really just means that the plants are grown in sufficient quantity and at a time and price that warrants them being grown en masse for temporary colour. Such plants are usually sold in trays or pots and, depending on the type, are available from six months before they are due to flower, right up until they have already started to do so.

When choosing them from a garden centre or shop, always look for healthy specimens. The ideal plant will not yet have started to flower, or have only a few flowers, which will mean that you have a full season of colour ahead of you. If they have already started blooming, the plants will have developed a significant root system and may respond badly when planted out. You will also have missed some of the flowering potential.

Most annual types will be tender (in that they will be damaged by frost or very cold weather). These plants, which will have been started off in a greenhouse, will need to be slowly acclimatized to colder conditions – a term that is known as 'hardening off' – then planted out once all danger of frost has passed.

Try to do as little damage to the roots and stems as possible when you remove the plants from their container. Damaged leaves will readily be replaced with new leaves, but a plant has only one stem!

LEFT *Vibrant colours can be provided for the summer by assorted annuals and bedding plants.*

Phlox '21st Century Pink'

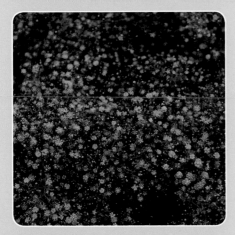
Gypsophila elegans

Begonia 'Stara Mixed'

■ Annual phlox (*Phlox drummondii*)

The annual phlox give a succession of colour throughout summer and are very easy to look after. Look for '21st Century Pink' (bright sugar pink), 'Twinkle Stars' (magenta and white) and 'Carnival' (a strain with flowers of pink, rose, salmon, scarlet, blue and violet). **USDA Zone:** Z6

■ Baby's breath, or chalk plant

(*Gypsophila elegans*)

This hardy annual thrives in any good garden soil, although it tends to prefer chalk. It is loved by flower arrangers as well as gardeners for its long-lasting, wispy, airy flowers, which come in white, pink or lilac. **USDA Zone:** Z5

■ Bedding, or wax begonia

(*Begonia semperflorens*)

This is the fibrous-rooted bedding begonia, as opposed to the tuberous-rooted container or house-plant type. Plants are usually 8–12in (20–30cm) high and have bronze or green leaves. Flowers come in shades of red, pink and white, and appear from early summer to late autumn. **USDA Zone:** Z9–11

■ Bells of Ireland (*Molucella laevis*)

This plant, which is tolerant of both wind and salt, has tiny, inconspicuous flowers. However, they are surrounded by a curious, light green calyx, which gives the plant a cool, green look that goes well with lots of hot, vibrant-coloured flowers. When the seeds form, these green calyces turn papery and light brown. **USDA Zone:** Z7

■ Blanket flower (*Gaillardia* spp)

This bright, daisy-flowered annual blooms for four months from mid summer onwards. Look for 'Sunburst Yellow with Red' (which perfectly describes the colours), 'Burgundy' (with flowers of burgundy red) and 'Sundance' (with deep red, double, almost globular flowers). **USDA Zone:** Z8

■ Busy Lizzie (*Impatiens* spp) This is an extremely popular, low-growing, highly floriferous, summer bedding plant. Flowers come in a variety of colours from white and pale pink through to oranges, deep reds and near purple. There is a new strain, called 'Sunpatiens', which is the first *Impatiens* variety to be both yellow and a sun-lover. Another interesting variety is 'Swirl Pink Improved'. **USDA Zone:** Z10

Molucella laevis

Gaillardia 'Sunburst Yellow with Red'

Impatiens 'Swirl Pink Improved'

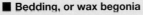

ANNUALS AND BEDDING PLANTS FOR COLOUR | **153**

Eschscholzia californica

Celosia plumosa (red and yellow hybrids)

Cosmos 'Dream Picotee'

■ **Californian poppy** (*Eschscholzia californica*)
This is the state flower of California and it grows beautifully all along the Pacific coastline. It blooms throughout the summer, the silky-textured flowers looking like orange, red-orange, rose-pink, warm yellow or cream poppies. There are also forms with attractively marked petals. **USDA Zone:** Z6

■ **Cockscomb** (*Celosia argentea*)
This makes an excellent specimen plant for a container, but it can also be used successfully in bedding schemes, if planted in quantity. The flowers appear as dense, feathery plumes. These are the Plumosa types, but there are also the Cristata types, which have crested flowers and are best as pot plants. **USDA Zone:** Z9

■ **Cosmos** (*Cosmos bipinnatus*)
This is a showy annual for the summer and early autumn. The daisy-like blooms can be single, double or crested, and usually come as white, pink, crimson or lavender, often with notched or frilled petals, and with yellow centres. 'Dream Picotee' is an excellent, free-flowering strain. **USDA Zone:** Z10

■ **Dianthus** (*Dianthus*)
There are many types of *Dianthus*, including perennials and biennials, as well as annual strains, such as 'Musical Score'. This is one of the newer forms, with very dark brown and white flowers; most *Dianthus* come in shades of red, orange, pink or white. These plants tolerate dappled shade and full sun, and acid and alkaline soils. Being low-growing – usually 12–24in (30–60cm) – they do not get blown over in windy gardens. **USDA Zone:** Z5–8

■ **Everlasting flower** (*Helichrysum bracteatum*)
We have already met one *Helichrysum* for coastal gardens (*H. petiolare* on p143). This form is entirely different, however. Everlasting flowers are brightly coloured, rather like miniature dahlias, and look as if they are made from paper. **USDA Zone:** Z10

■ **Floss flower** (*Ageratum houstonianum*)
A perfect plant for edging a flower bed or border, *Ageratum* is well known for its fluffy, powder-blue flowers. There are also pink and white forms, but these are much less popular. *A. houstonianum* 'Blue Mink' and 'High Tide Blue' provide some of the clearest of blues. **USDA Zone:** Z10

Dianthus 'Musical Score'

Helichrysum 'Visual Golden Yellow'

Ageratum 'High Tide Blue'

Heliotropium arborescens 'P.K. Lowther'

Mesembryanthemum 'Gelato Orange'

Nigella 'Miss Jekyll' AGM

■ **Heliotrope, or cherry pie**
(*Heliotropium arborescens*)
These flowers, which really do smell of cherry pie, come in purple, violet-blue or white and appear from early summer until mid autumn. 'Marine' (wine-purple) and 'P.K. Lowther' (pale purple) are excellent forms. **USDA Zone:** Z10

■ **Livingstone daisy** (*Mesembryanthemum* spp)
This is a succulent plant with masses of daisy flowers in shades of red, pink, white, orange, yellow and cream. The flowers open fully when the sun is out and tend to close during cloudy weather. Being a ground-hugger means that it is ideal for gardens right at the edge of the sea. **USDA Zone:** Z9

■ **Love-in-a-Mist** (*Nigella damascena*)
If you want a plant that produces masses of dainty, blue flowers from early summer to autumn, and you have a sunny spot on a free-draining soil, then this is for you. Look for 'Miss Jekyll' (bright blue) AGM, 'Oxford Blue' (very dark blue) and *Nigella papillosa* 'Midnight' (a rich, dark purple). **USDA Zone:** Z7

■ **Nasturtium** (*Tropaeolum majus*)
These annuals can smother other plants if left to run wild, but they do carry fine flowers in orange, red and yellow. They do not mind salty air and, because of their twining habit, do not come unstuck when the wind blows. The Alaska Series AGM is popular, but the Jewel and Whirlybird Series are equally as good. **USDA Zone:** Z9

■ **Pelargonium** (*Geranium* spp)
There are hundreds of varieties of pelargonium, perhaps better known as the bedding geranium. They all love the warm, clear air and sunshine of the coastal garden. These are actually tender perennial plants and, with care, they can be kept from year to year. Some of the more interesting forms in recent years are those with decorative foliage, such as 'Black Magic Red F1'. **USDA Zone:** Z10

■ **Persian shield** (*Strobilanthes dyerianus*)
This is not an annual, nor even a perennial in the true sense of the word: it is actually a soft-stemmed shrub that is best grown as an annual. It is very tender, being native to Burma, but if successfully kept over winter it will be evergreen. It is grown for its attractive dark purple leaves. **USDA Zone:** Z10

Tropaeolum majus 'Tip Top Alaska Red'

Geranium 'Black Magic Red F1'

Strobilanthes dyerianus 'Persian Shield'

Petunia 'Ramblin Mixed F1'

Lantana 'Lucky Red Hot'

■ **Petunia** (*Petunia* spp)
These rank probably as the most popular summer bedding plant of all, with hundreds of varieties available. Petunias bloom best in a sunny and warm position and they flower continuously until cut down by the first frosts. There are miniatures, ground creepers, trailers and twiners, so they will suit many areas of your coastal garden. **USDA Zone:** Z7

■ **Pot marigold** (*Calendula* spp)
The pot marigold is a hardy annual that can be sown in autumn for flowering the following summer. Its bright flowers work extremely well by the sea. Look for 'Daisy Mixed' (golden yellow, orange and cream) and 'Art Shades Mixed' (apricot, orange and cream). **USDA Zone:** Z6

■ **Salvia** (*Salvia patens*)
There are annual and perennial salvias. Some perennials are better grown as annuals, though – and this is the case with *Salvia patens*. Upright, branching plants have mid-green leaves and attractive flowers in different shades of blue. Look for 'Blue Angel' (a rich royal blue) and 'Cambridge Blue AGM' (light blue). **USDA Zone:** Z8

■ **Shrubby verbena** (*Lantana* spp)
These sub-shrubs are best grown as low-growing annuals to be discarded at the end of the summer, or kept in a greenhouse over winter to become larger shrubs growing to 6ft (2m) or so. There are several reds, yellows and oranges available such as 'Lucky Red Hot'. **USDA Zone:** Z10

■ **Signet marigold** (*Tagetes tenuifolia*)
The *Tagetes* genus is best known for its large-flowered French and African marigolds. Better suited to a coastal garden, however, are the ferny-leaved, smaller-flowered strains of *Tagetes tenuifolia*. These plants form many-branched clumps some 15in (37cm) high and they have a strong fragrance. Try 'Luna Golden Yellow'. **USDA Zone:** Z9

■ **Snapdragon** (*Antirrhinum majus*)
This is a versatile summer bedding plant, being good in beds, borders and containers. It is actually a tender perennial and in some gardens will survive from year to year. The dwarf kinds are better for exposed coastal gardens. Look for 'Montego Mix F1' and the trailing 'Pearly Queen Mix'. **USDA Zone:** Z7

Calendula 'Daisy Mixed'

Tagetes 'Luna Golden Yellow'

Salvia patens 'Blue Angel'

Antirrhinum majus 'Montego Mix F1'

Cleome spinosa 'Pink Queen'

Portulaca 'Tequila Mix'

Brachycome iberidifolia

■ **Spider flower** (*Cleome hassleriana*)
The curious bloom of this summer-flowering annual plant really does have spidery qualities. Usually rose-purple, pink or white, the flowers come loosely clustered at the tops of stems, with 'legs' coming out at all angles. It is a tall plant at 4–5ft (1.2–1.5m), so place near the back of the border. **USDA Zone:** Z10

■ **Sun plant, or rose moss** (*Portulaca* spp)
This is a succulent plant, producing creeping stems that cover the ground. It is a sun-lover, but does not grow higher than about 6in (15cm), so it is good for a windy garden. It flowers throughout summer, producing small, rose-like blooms in whites, yellows, oranges, reds and pinks. A modern strain is 'Tequila Mix'. **USDA Zone:** Z9

■ **Swan river daisy** (*Brachycome iberidifolia*)
This white daisy flower is entirely suited to coastal gardens and it flowers from late spring to early autumn. 'Dwarf Bravo Mixed' is lower-growing than the main species, reaching just 10in (25cm) or so, with flowers in shades of blue, violet and white, with black or yellow centres. 'Purple Splendour' (purple blue) is also excellent. **USDA Zone:** Z8

■ **Tickseed** (*Coreopsis* spp)
Although perennials, these flower in the first year from seed, so are often grown as annuals. They have bright, daisy flowers and enjoy being grown in a sunny border where they will flower profusely during mid summer. Look for the shorter varieties, such as 'Sunfire' (deep yellow and maroon), 'Zagreb' AGM (gold yellow) and 'Mahogany Midget' (deep red). **USDA Zone:** Z4–9

■ **Treasure flower** (*Gazania* spp)
With large, bright, daisy flowers, there is little to surpass these plants for brilliance and colour when the sun shines. Although the prominent colours are shades of orange, breeders have created different coloured zones within the flowers. **USDA Zone:** Z9

■ **Verbena** (*Verbena* x *hybrida*)
With the introduction of many different colours and weather tolerance, as well as prolonged flowering, verbenas have become much more fashionable. A good example is 'Tukana Hot Pink and Salmon mixed with Raspberry'. They can be grown as annuals for summer use. **USDA Zone:** Z9

Coreopsis 'Sunfire'

Gazania 'Daybreak Bronze'

Verbena x hybrida 'Tukana Hot Pink'

Chapter 14

GROUND COVER PLANTS

 Ground cover plants do exactly what their name suggests – they grow along the ground, smothering weeds in their wake. They can, in an ideal situation, cover every bit of available soil so that you are hard-pressed to see the bare earth (if you can, it means that weeds can grow there too).

RIGHT *'Shinglesea' was a coastal-style garden created by garden designer Chris O'Donaghue for the 2007 Chelsea Flower Show, in London, UK.*

Ground cover plants

There is an enormous range of ground cover plants. They come in all of the common hardy plant genres; they may be herbaceous, shrubby, woody, succulent or grass-like. In addition, they may have a clumping, sprawling or vining habit, and may be evergreen (the most useful) or they can be deciduous, or somewhere in between. There are even forms that are annual, biennial or perennial by nature.

Ground coverers are the perfect choice if you have an awkward bank of soil that is unsuitable for grassing over, either because it makes subsequent mowing dangerous or because the slope is such that the soil and grass are unstable.

They are also excellent for dryish soil in shade, such as under a tree. And they come into their own if you have a large area and little time to look after it – for these plants, in general, look after themselves. For the most part, ground cover plants can be anywhere between 1in (2.5cm) and 4ft (1.2m) high, and you can choose from plain green types (some may say 'boring'), to those that are excitingly colourful and vibrant.

Those discussed on the next few pages are all suitable for growing in coastal gardens, with a few even being happy along the seashore.

LEFT This exotic planting has tall trees providing the canopy – but under this is a range of lower-growing ground cover plants.

Aubrieta 'Hartswood Purple'

Persicaria amplexicaulis 'Firetail' AGM

Pachysandra terminalis

■ **Aubrieta** (*Aubrieta* spp)

This hardy, evergreen perennial has masses of small, four-petalled spring flowers in shades of pink, mauve, purple, blue and white. Perfect for the rock garden, or on scree slopes or dry walls, it will survive close to the sea. There are several forms, such as 'Hartswood Purple'. **USDA Zone:** Z5–8

■ **Bistort, or knotweed** (*Persicaria* spp)

This is a huge family, which includes the famously invasive Japanese knotweed. However, there are some non-invasive forms that are ideal for coastal gardens. All are sturdy and attractive perennials

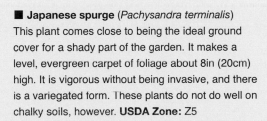

amplexicaulis 'Firetail' AGM. **USDA Zone:** Z4–8

■ **Japanese spurge** (*Pachysandra terminalis*)

This plant comes close to being the ideal ground cover for a shady part of the garden. It makes a level, evergreen carpet of foliage about 8in (20cm) high. It is vigorous without being invasive, and there is a variegated form. These plants do not do well on chalky soils, however. **USDA Zone:** Z5

■ **Blue flaky juniper** (*Juniperus squamata*)

This plain species is tall and not really suited to gardens, but it has produced some first-class cultivars, including 'Blue Carpet', which is a very vigorous spreading plant. The outer branches have attractively nodding tips. In winter the foliage colour can be purplish, steel blue or blue green, whilst in summer it is much more silvery. **USDA Zone:** Z5

■ **Broom** (*Genista tinctoria*)

This is a sun-loving, drought-tolerant plant that will positively thrive in the free-draining, sandy soil of a garden close to the shoreline. Its bright yellow pea flowers last for several weeks in early summer, and the double form, 'Flore Pleno' AGM, is even better. *Genista lydia* AGM is a low, spreading form also, but better for a rock garden. **USDA Zone:** Z5–9

■ **Bugle** (*Ajuga reptans*)

A hardy perennial with creeping stems, this vigorous, plant can be a nuisance. It flowers well in summer, producing blue spikes around 6in (15cm) in height; however, the foliage is often the most important feature. 'Burgundy Glow' has maroon and cream leaves, 'Braunherz' AGM is deep purple and bronze, and 'Variegata' is green and cream. **USDA Zone:** Z6

Juniperus squamata 'Blue Carpet'

Genista tinctoria 'Flore Pleno' AGM

Ajuga reptans 'Variegata'

Ceanothus 'Blue Mound' AGM

Hedera canariensis 'Gloire de Marengo' AGM

Geranium 'Russell Prichard' AGM

■ **Californian lilac** (*Ceanothus* spp)
The *Ceanothus* shown on page 132 is an upright form, and there are many that make tall shrubs for growing against walls. There are just as many low-growing forms that cover the ground, effectively turning it blue when they are in flower. One of the best is 'Blue Mound' AGM. **USDA Zone:** Z4–8

■ **Canary Island ivy** (*Hedera canariensis*)
Although less often grown than the common ivy (*Hedera helix*), the Canary Island ivy is a more striking plant, especially in the form 'Gloire de Marengo' AGM. Its leaves are marbled with white, giving it lots of impact. Although it is generally regarded as a foliage climber, it will also carpet a large area of ground. **USDA Zone:** Z8

■ **Cranesbill, or hardy geranium** (*Geranium* spp)
These are generally clump-forming plants, with lobed or divided green leaves, and summer flowers in shades of white, pink, purple and blue. There are hundreds of forms – all are very hardy and all are accepting of wind and salty air. The cultivar 'Russell Prichard' AGM freely produces deep pink flowers. **USDA Zone:** Z6

■ **Dead-nettle** (*Lamium* spp)
We have already seen the silver-leaved *Lamium* (p142), but there are many forms and all are good ground coverers. *L. orvala* is arguably the species that most closely resembles the nettle (*Urtica* spp). This form produces clusters of pink flowers during late spring and early summer. **USDA Zone:** Z6

■ **Elephant's ears** (*Bergenia* spp)
These evergreen perennials are low, spreading plants with glossy leaves that contrast well with other foliage. They make excellent ground cover. The nodding clusters of bell-shaped flowers are most attractive in late winter and spring. Both foliage and flowers are good for cutting. **USDA Zone:** Z3

■ **Thrift, or sea pink** (*Armeria maritima*)
A small, clump-forming perennial, this plant grows to about 8in (20cm) high. It produces a basal mound of narrow, grassy, dark green leaves, and in late spring and early summer it sends out spherical heads of rose-pink, pink or white flowers on stiff, slender stems. The most important thing for this plant is a free-draining soil. **USDA Zone:** Z4

Lamium orvala

Bergenia 'Pugsley's Pink'

Armeria maritima

Viburnum davidii AGM

Liriope muscari AGM

Calluna 'Forest Fire'

■ **Evergreen viburnum** (*Viburnum davidii* AGM)
The extensive use of this plant shows its versatility and appeal. It is at its best when it is still young, forming a compact mound of deep green, curiously veined leaves. Near a male pollinator, female plants produce stunning winter berries, described variously as blue-black and turquoise. **USDA Zone:** Z7

■ **Lilyturf** (*Liriope muscari* AGM)
This is a tough but graceful plant. It develops a clump of narrow, grass-like, evergreen leaves about 12in (30cm) high. In autumn, plants send up slender spikes of tiny, round purple flowers that are often followed by small black berries. It seems to thrive in gardens very close to the sea. **USDA Zone:** Z6

■ **Heather (i)** (*Calluna* spp)
This is a well-known ground cover plant for an acid soil. Although it flowers best in full sun, it does tolerate some shade. The flowers come in shades of white, pink, red and lilac in the summer and early autumn, and many forms have attractive winter and early spring foliage. 'Forest Fire' also has red tips to the young spring foliage. **USDA Zone:** Z4

■ **Heather (ii)** (*Erica carnea*)
This can be very successful near the sea. It is rarely troubled by salt or wind – which just blow over the top of it. Dark green, needle-like, evergreen leaves are topped in late winter or early spring by masses of tiny, tubular flowers. Look for 'King George' (dark pink), 'Myretoun Ruby' AGM (ruby red) and 'Springwood White' AGM (white). **USDA Zone:** Z5

■ **x Heucherella** (*Heucherella* spp)
These are hybrids between *Heuchera* and *Tiarella* – and they are thought by many to be superior plants. They are profuse and repeat bloomers, with little starry flowers on thin stems. 'Tapestry' has stunning, multicoloured leaves with dark centres, and warm pink flowers. **USDA Zone:** Z5

■ **Houseleek** (*Sempervivum* spp)
These creeping succulents will grow across the ground, but do not grow them if you want something to smother weeds, as these are too slow and too sparse. They are highly decorative, however, and incredibly tough plants. They need so little water and nutrients that they can grow perfectly well from a pocket of soil in a stone wall. **USDA Zone:** Z4–8

Erica carnea 'King George'

x Heucherella 'Tapestry'

Sempervivum 'Bloodtip'

Chapter 15

CLIMBERS AND
WALL PLANTS

In every garden, whether it is within sight of the sea or situated hundreds of miles inland, there is a vertical surface somewhere that could be covered by a plant. This could transform the garden from one that looks bare, with hard lines of fence and wall, into something that is horticulturally delightful.

RIGHT *In any setting, plants growing at height (such as on trelliswork panels and pergolas) bring an added dimension to the garden.*

Climbers and wall plants

Climbing plants provide the gardener with the means of adorning walls, fences and other structures such as pergolas with flowers and foliage. They can add charm and individuality to a building – be it a house, garage or even a humble garden shed – and they are great for obscuring unsightly views. Walls, of course, are particularly good for growing climbers against because they provide shelter and warmth, so you may find that you are able to grow some plants from warmer climates.

Climbing plants really come into their own in small gardens. They do not take up valuable ground space, so they still allow gardeners to enjoy and practise the hobby, regardless of what the dimensions of the garden are.

There is no great secret to growing good climbers. They need a well-prepared soil, as well as occasional feeding, watering and general nurturing, and perhaps a bit of pruning, just like any other plant. They may, however, also need occasional tying in to supports, wires, canes or trelliswork, especially in windy coastal gardens.

This chapter does not include climbing and rambling plants exclusively. There are also a number of 'wall plants' – shrubs that are at their best when grown in proximity to a wall. In cooler or temperate gardens, plants such as the germander, oleander and the Chilean potato vine will be at risk of suffering from exposure if they are not grown in the lee of a wall. So whilst they do not use the wall for support, as do true climbing plants, the structure is just as important to them, but for different reasons.

LEFT Climbing and rambling plants can be trained to walls and wires, or, as seen here, left to scramble over structures.

Abelia x grandiflora AGM

Parthenocissus tricuspidata AGM

■ **Abelia** (*Abelia* x *grandiflora* AGM)
This vigorous, rounded shrub can be evergreen or semi-evergreen and grows to around 6½ft (2m) high and across. It does best near a wall. The glossy, dark green leaves are accompanied by pink, white and lilac trumpet-like flowers from mid summer to mid autumn. **USDA Zone:** Z5

■ **Actinidia** (*Actinidia kolomikta* AGM)
A non-vigorous, deciduous climber from China and Japan, *Actinidia* is closely related to the Kiwi fruit, or Chinese gooseberry. When fully developed, the leaves have a large area of pink and white at the tips, which looks as though they have been dipped in paint. **USDA Zone:** Z4

■ **Black-eyed Susan** (*Thunbergia alata*)
A twining annual, this plant has heart-shaped, mid-green leaves and showy, usually orange-yellow flowers with a long, dark brown tube, giving them a 'black-eyed' appearance. Flowers are carried from early to late summer. **USDA Zone:** Z10

■ **Boston ivy** (*Parthenocissus tricuspidata* AGM)
This covers a house wall in fiery reds, golds, oranges, yellows and purples in autumn. Its deep blue berries after leaf fall are relished by birds. Two alternatives are *P. henryana* AGM, with dark, purplish-green, deeply lobed leaves turning to the bright colours in autumn, and the true Virginia creeper (*P. quinquefolia* AGM), with leaves composed of five oval leaflets. **USDA Zone:** Z3–7

■ **Camellia** (*Camellia* spp)
We have seen how the Camellia can make a wonderful springtime shrub (page 132), but it is originally a woodland plant, so it does not perform well in exposed gardens or in an open, very sunny spot. It makes a good plant for the lee of a wall, preferably facing north, south or west. If the wall is east-facing, the early morning sun on a cold day can cause the camellia flowers to go brown and drop, by thawing the flowers too quickly. **USDA Zone:** Z8

■ **Cape leadwort** (*Plumbago auriculata* AGM)
This is a fast-growing, evergreen, woody-stemmed, scrambling climber. It is equally at home growing along wires and into trees, as well as climbing over banks. Trusses of sky-blue flowers are produced from summer to early winter. **USDA Zone:** Z9

Actinidia kolomikta AGM

Camellia 'Empire Rose'

Thunbergia alata

Plumbago auriculata AGM

Solanum crispum 'Glasnevin' AGM

Clematis montana var. rubens

Clematis flammula

■ **Chilean potato vine** (*Solanum crispum*) This scrambling, semi-evergreen shrub is usually seen growing up a wall or fence. The bluish-purple, star-shaped flowers, which appear from early to late summer, have prominent, deep yellow anthers. The cultivar 'Glasnevin' AGM has flowers that continue into early autumn. **USDA Zone:** Z8

■ **Clematis** (*Clematis* spp)
Known as the 'Queen of Climbers', there are hundreds of types of *Clematis* to choose from, and their flower colours range from white to deep purples, with every colour in between save for the orange shades. It is difficult to choose between them all, but if you had to take just one on your imaginary desert island, it probably should be *Clematis montana* var *rubens*; in late spring it just fills every spare bit of space, for about three weeks, with pale pink flowers. It can be left to ramble over buildings or up into trees. *C. flammula*, meanwhile, is a vigorous form with masses of almond-scented, flattish, single flowers from early summer to late autumn. *C. tangutica*, from central Asia, produces yellow, lantern-shaped flowers from mid summer to mid autumn; these are followed by decorative, silky seedheads. **USDA Zone:** Z6 (*C. tangutica* Z5)

■ **Climbing hydrangea**
(*Hydrangea petiolaris* AGM)
This climber will cover a large area, its white and cream flowerheads appearing profusely even on a shady, cold wall. It produces attractive, deep green foliage that turns to bright yellow in autumn, and large, flat, white blossom clusters in summer. It needs plenty of moisture during the first year or two after planting, but thereafter becomes quite drought-tolerant. **USDA Zone:** Z5

■ **Climbing or rambling rose** (*Rosa* spp)
There are seemingly hundreds of climbing roses to choose from, and some can have vicious thorns, so it pays not to grow them really close to paths and patios. However, you do not want them to be too far away either, as the flower fragrances can be fantastic. Four favourites include 'Pink Perpétué' (pink), 'Golden Showers' AGM (yellow), 'Dortmund' AGM (deep pink and white) and the modern climber 'Sir John Mills'. **USDA Zone:** Z2–9

Clematis tangutica

Hydrangea petiolaris AGM

Rosa 'Sir John Mills'

Trachelospermum jasminoides AGM

Cobaea scandens AGM

Olearia x scilloniensis AGM

■ **Confederate jasmine** (*Trachelospermum jasminoides* AGM)

This evergreen vine acquired its common name from its long history of being grown in gardens of the southeastern states of the US. It grows to 15ft (4.5m) or more, and has small, dark green, glossy leaves, which turn red in the autumn. In spring and early summer, it carries clusters of fragrant, star-shaped flowers of creamy white. **USDA Zone:** Z9

■ **Cup and saucer vine, or Mexican ivy** (*Cobaea scandens* AGM)

This is a tender perennial that is usually treated as an annual. It is a quick grower, using tendrils to haul itself up supports each year. It will reach 30ft (9m) if left alone. Purple, bell-shaped flowers with prominent stamens appear from late spring to the first frosts of autumn. **USDA Zone:** Z9

■ **Daisy bush** (*Olearia* x *scilloniensis* AGM)

The chief attraction of this evergreen shrub from Australasia is the clusters of white, daisy-like flowers in late spring and early summer. This particular natural hybrid was discovered on the Isles of Scilly, just off the southwest corner of England – where conditions could not be more coastal. It reaches a height of 4ft (1.2m) and has serrated, grey-green leaves, white felted beneath. **USDA Zone:** Z8

■ **Firethorn** (*Pyracantha* spp)

The firethorns are evergreen shrubs that have spiny branches and usually produce a profusion of small, bright, summer flowers. These are followed by large numbers of autumn berries in yellow and orange (page 137). They all make fine wall shrubs and hedging plants. **USDA Zone:** Z6–8

■ **Flowering honeysuckle** (*Lonicera* spp)

The honeysuckles are grown chiefly for their fragrant flowers, but they are also vigorous ramblers. If you have space to grow them, they are fabulous. Just take a close-up look at the intricacy of the flower – you'll be amazed. **USDA Zone:** Z2–9

■ **Germander** (*Teucrium* spp)

This genus contains perennials and shrubs mostly from the Mediterranean region. Several, such as *T. hircanicum* and *T. chamaedrys*, make lovely wall plants. Flowers in rose-purple spikes are carried from mid- to late summer. **USDA Zone:** Z4–9

Pyracantha (Firethorn)

Lonicera x italica

Teucrium 'Purple Tails'

Abutilon vitifolium 'Tennant's White' AGM

Vitis coignetiae AGM

Nerium oleander

■ **Indian mallow** (*Abutilon vitifolium*)

The Indian mallow (actually from Chile) is an upright shrub that needs the protection of a wall if it is to do well. The maple-like leaves are grey-green and softly hairy, whilst the white, early summer flowers are five-petalled and saucer-shaped. **USDA Zone:** Z8

■ **Japanese crimson glory vine**

(*Vitis coignetiae* AGM)

This deciduous, climbing plant grows to a height and spread of up to 82ft (25m) or so, but it can be pruned annually to be kept smaller. Thick, lobed, pale green leaves up to 12in (30cm) across turn to shades of gold, orange and purple-red in autumn. Green flowers in mid-spring are followed by barely edible purple-black fruits. **USDA Zone:** Z5

■ **Oleander** (*Nerium oleander*)

This is an upright, bushy, evergreen shrub that is frequently used as a potted plant for the conservatory or sun room. If grown outdoors in a temperate climate, it needs to be in full sun and protected by a wall. Clusters of pink, white, red, apricot or yellow flowers appear from spring to autumn, often on dark red stalks. **USDA Zone:** Z8

■ **Ozothamnus** (*Ozothamnus rosmarinifolius*)

Another upright, evergreen shrub, *Ozothamnus* has dense, woolly, white shoots and narrow leaves of deep green. The fragrant, white, early summer flowers come in clustered heads. **USDA Zone:** Z8

■ **Passion flower** (*Passiflora caerulea* AGM)

This is the common, or blue, hardy passion flower. It is a vigorous climber with a dense habit. It has a height and spread of 20–30ft (6–9m) and carries light to mid-green lobed leaves. Slightly scented, white and blue-purple flowers are produced from early summer to early autumn. The variety 'Constance Elliott' is ivory white. **USDA Zone:** Z7

■ **Persian ivy, or Colchis ivy** (*Hedera colchica* AGM)

Many people hate ivies, believing them to be a pest. In fact, they do real damage to a building only if the brickwork is already unsound. The variety of forms means that there is probably one that you'll like. *Hedera colchica* is a useful garden ivy, but it tends to be overshadowed by its larger-leaved and more vigorous clone 'Dentata' AGM. A popular, variegated form is 'Sulphur Heart' AGM. **USDA Zone:** Z6

Ozothamnus rosmarinifolius

Passiflora caerulea AGM

Hedera colchica 'Sulphur Heart' AGM

Hibiscus rosa-sinensis

Lathyrus 'Pastel Sunset'

Leptospermum lanigerum

■ **Rose of China** (*Hibiscus rosa-sinensis*)
The *Hibiscus* is a large genus of annuals, and evergreen and deciduous shrubs. The Rose of China is an attractive plant best grown in the shelter of a sunny wall. In cold areas, overwinter it in a pot in a frost-free greenhouse or conservatory. Flowers come in a wide range of colours. **USDA Zone:** Z9

■ **Sweet pea** (*Lathyrus* spp)
These familiar, annual climbers are sown in autumn or spring for flowering the following summer. The pea flowers have the nicest of scents. There are dozens of varieties and most will grow happily up and along supports. **USDA Zone:** Z5

■ **Ti tree, or tea tree** (*Leptospermum* spp)
The *Leptospermum* is a genus of evergreen trees and shrubs grown for their leaf decoration and small, often profuse flowering. Although perhaps not the most attractive of garden plants, they are particularly suited to coastal gardens, provided that the position is sunny and the soil well drained. *L. lanigerum* can eventually make a tree 17ft (5m) or so high, but it appreciates wall protection. **USDA Zone:** Z8–9

■ **Trumpet vine** (*Campsis* spp)
These perennial climbers produce scarlet and orange (or sometimes yellow) trumpet-like flowers in summer. They are drought-tolerant and are happy in full sun or partial shade. Watch out for the vines growing into openings – windows, eaves, gutters etc. These are very hardy and can be grown close to the seashore. **USDA Zone:** Z4

■ **Winter jasmine** (*Jasminum nudiflorum* AGM)
This is a hardy, deciduous, rambling plant, growing to around 10–15ft (3–4.5m). It needs to have a sturdy wall to clamber over. Bright yellow flowers grow along bare, green stems from late autumn until mid winter. **USDA Zone:** Z6

■ **Wisteria** (*Wisteria* spp)
Wisteria sinensis is arguably the grandest climber of them all. It originates from China, and many who have grown it wish it had stayed there. During its peak season, it can send shoots up into a tree or neighbours' gardens in a few weeks. Prune in mid winter and in high summer to keep it under control. The highly scented, large, lilac-coloured flower clusters are utterly ravishing. **USDA Zone:** Z4–8

Campsis x tagliabuana 'Madame Galen' AGM

Jasminum nudiflorum AGM

Wisteria sinensis

Chapter 16

BEST PLANTS
FOR SHADE

 Coastal gardens generally have plenty of 'sky'; it is the exposure to sunshine and daylight that brings many people to the coast in the first place. But every garden also contains shade at some point during the day, so which plants suited to the coastal climate can also withstand periods out of the sun?

RIGHT *Shade beds at Windcliff, Seattle, Washington State, US.*

Shade-tolerant plants

There is one inescapable fact in gardening – there will always be some shade somewhere in the garden. However, there are different types of shade. For example, it may cover a small or a large area; it may exist for a short period during the day or for most of it; and it may be heavy and dense shade with no impenetrable sunlight, or it may be light and dappled shade that merely filters sunlight. Most gardens, of course, have a combination of all these.

It is important to know which of your plants are most suited to shade because to put a sun-loving plant in an area of dense shade will be a waste of time, money and effort. The plant will not develop properly, it will look sickly and, if the production of flowers is the reason for growing it, you will be seriously disappointed.

Shade is not such a bad thing, however. It prevents plants from becoming scorched and it enables you to grow a different range of plants, giving your garden variety and diversity. It is also a useful area to sit out of the sun in hot weather!

There are plenty of plants to choose from, but in a coastal garden you still have to make sure that they are tolerant of salt and wind as well.

LEFT *Waterside and bog plants are frequently also shade-loving plants.*

Astilbe 'Bronce Elegans' AGM

■ **Astilbe** (*Astilbe simplicifolia*)

In a hot, dry garden the *Astilbe* is lacklustre and produces spindly flowers. With a light shade and a moist soil, however, they can be dramatic perennials for many weeks in the summer. There are dozens of varieties to choose from, with flowers ranging from white, through the pinks and reds, to maroon. One of the best is 'Bronce Elegans' AGM, with charming, blush-pink flowers and dark leaves. **USDA Zone:** Z6

■ **Bedding begonia, or wax begonia** (*Begonia semperflorens*)

The fibrous-rooted begonias, popular as summer bedding plants, are actually short-lived perennials that make good patio pot plants. There are dozens of varieties, one of the newest strains being the 'Blue Skies' range, in shades of pink and white. Dappled shade is preferred. **USDA Zone:** Z9–11

■ **Blueberry** (*Vaccinium* spp)

The blueberry is one of the few plants grown for its fruits that is suitable for a coastal garden and a shady one. It needs an acid soil that tends not to dry out. In the autumn the leaves turn to gold and yellow. A popular variety is 'Berkeley'. **USDA Zone:** Z6–8

■ **Butcher's broom** (*Ruscus aculeatus*)

This is a curious plant, for what appear to be its leaves are, in fact, flattened stems. Their waxy covering means that they are particularly tolerant of wind, salt and all that a coastal garden can throw at them. This plant can also tolerate quite dense shade. Red berries appear on female plants, but only if males are grown nearby. **USDA Zone:** Z7

■ **Chilean bamboo** (*Chusquea culeou* AGM)

This tall bamboo is ideal for dense shade. Plants grow to 12ft (3.6m), and they produce solid culms of green-yellow leaves and canes. It is best grown as a specimen plant in a lawn or at the back of a border. **USDA Zone:** Z7

■ **Coleus, or flame nettle** (*Solenostemon* spp)

Familiar, short-lived perennials grown as annuals, there are many excellent forms of coleuses, all grown for their brightly coloured leaves. If you nip out the flower spikes, you will prolong the period of foliage production and the plants will be more dramatic. The modern cultivar 'Kong Mosaic' has large, multicoloured leaves. **USDA Zone:** Z10

Begonia 'Blue Skies'

Vaccinium 'Berkeley'

Ruscus aculeatus

Chusquea culeou AGM

Solenostemon 'Kong Mosaic'

Ilex aquifolium AGM

Heuchera sanguinea 'Ruby Bells'

Corydalis flexuosa

■ **Common holly** (*Ilex aquifolium* AGM)
The common holly has many hybrids. The species has dark green leaves and red berries. However, there are forms with yellow berries ('Pyramidalis Fructu Luteo' AGM), and some with variegated leaves ('Golden Queen' AGM). All grow well by the sea, especially in light shade. **USDA Zone:** Z5–6

■ **Coral bells** (*Heuchera* spp)
Much breeding work has taken place with these plants, resulting in dozens of varieties being launched. Grown mainly for their coloured leaves, the wispy flowers on wiry stems are of secondary importance. Plant are from 6in (15cm) to 24in (60cm) in height. **USDA Zone:** Z4–9

■ **Corydalis** (*Corydalis flexuosa*)
This perennial has dark, finely cut foliage and blue-spurred flowers in spring. It is delicate-looking, but actually quite tough. It thrives in dappled to light shade and is therefore suitable for woodland gardens, as well as lightly shaded borders or rock and alpine gardens. **USDA Zone:** Z5

■ **Cotoneaster** (*Cotoneaster* spp)
There are a great many types of *Cotoneaster*, both evergreen and deciduous. Most need a sunny spot, but there are a few that prefer dappled to light shade. *C. conspicuus* grows to a height of just 12in (30cm), but can spread out to as much as 6–10ft (2–3m). Small, red-scarlet or orange-red berries are produced in autumn. Look out also for the herringbone cotoneaster (*C. horizontalis* AGM) (page 137). **USDA Zone:** Z6

■ **Cranesbill, or hardy geranium** (*Geranium psilostemon* AGM)
Geraniums are generally thought of as sun-lovers, but there are a number that prefer dappled light. One such is *G. psilostemon*, with bright, magenta flowers. It can easily reach 4ft (1.2m) in height, so it is best sited towards the back of a border. **USDA Zone:** Z6

■ **Forget-me-not** (*Myosotis* spp)
This popular, blue, biennial plant does not like the sun much; in fact it can thrive in quite dense shade. There are several excellent cultivars – look for 'Blue Ball' AGM with flowers of bright blue and 'Bobo Mixed' with flowers of blue, pink and white appearing on different plants. **USDA Zone:** Z4–8

Cotoneaster conspicuus

Geranium psilostemon AGM

Myosotis (forget-me-not)

Lunaria annua 'Variegata'

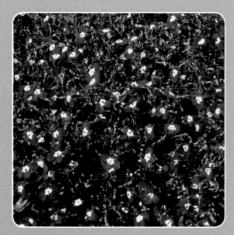

Lobelia 'Regatta Marine Blue'

Aconitum japonicum

■ **Honesty** (*Lunaria annua*)

This biennial plant produces bright purple or white, summer flowers. These are followed by round, flat, parchment-like seed pods that are popular with flower arrangers. It grows very well in coastal gardens in dappled shade. Try 'Variegata', with cream-white leaf markings. **USDA Zone:** Z6–8

■ **Lobelia** (*Lobelia* spp)

Bedding lobelias prefer to be grown in light shade. These plants are valued for their low-growing blue, purple, crimson and white flowers. There are many forms, both trailing and low-growing, but 'Regatta Marine Blue' works particularly well in coastal situations. **USDA Zone:** Z7

■ **Monkshood** (*Aconitum japonicum*)

The distinctive, hooded flowers of this plant have given rise to its common name of monkshood. Deep violet-blue, summer flowers really stand out against the vivid green of the leaves. Light or dappled shade will prolong the flowering season. All parts are poisonous, especially the roots. **USDA Zone:** Z6

■ **Oak-leafed hydrangea**

(*Hydrangea quercifolia* AGM)

This is one of the most underrated of shrubs. It is architecturally valuable, with bold, lobed leaves that are similar to oak, though larger – for example, in the variety 'Snow Queen'. Conical, white flowerheads appear in late summer, and it also produces fine autumn colours. The shrub grows to around 4ft (1.2m) in height. **USDA Zone:** Z5

■ **Oregon grape** (*Mahonia aquifolium*)

The *Mahonia* has long been a popular, winter-flowering, evergreen shrub, with its stiff stems, strange leaf arrangements and primrose-yellow flowers that can appear at any time from late autumn to early spring. *M. aquifolium* produces rather dense flower clusters in bright yellow. **USDA Zone:** Z5

■ **Plantain lily** (*Hosta* spp)

Grown principally for their handsome foliage, which is produced in a range of shapes, sizes and colours, hostas also carry strong stems of mostly lilac or white trumpet-shaped flowers during summer. Watch out for slugs and snails, which devour the leaves. There are hundreds of species and hybrids, for example, the cultivar 'Antioch'. **USDA Zone:** Z3

Hydrangea quercifolia 'Snow Queen'

Mahonia aquifolium

Hosta 'Antioch'

Rhododendron 'Loderi Group'

Rodgersia 'Kupfermond'

Sasa veitchii

■ **Rhododendron** (*Rhododendron* spp)
Rhododendrons are spectacular garden plants.
Most types flower in spring, although there are
a few, such as the white-flowering cultivar 'Polar
Bear', that flower in mid winter. Their natural habitat
is woodland, so they enjoy filtered sunlight. Their
thick, often felted leaves are resistant to wind and
salt – but they need neutral to acid soil; otherwise
confine them to containers. A lovely pink variety is
Rhododendron 'Loderi Group'. **USDA Zone:** Z5–9

■ **Rodgersia** (*Rodgersia* spp)
This is one of those perennial garden plants that
looks best next to a pond or woodland stream, but
incongruous anywhere else. In mid summer, plumes
of many tiny pinkish-red blossoms are held well
above the foliage. The cultivar 'Kupfermond' has
large heads of blush pink. **USDA Zone:** Z5

■ **Sasa** (*Sasa veitchii*)
This broad-leaved bamboo has distinctive pale
edges to its leaves, not because the foliage is
variegated, but due to the withdrawal of colour from
the current year's leaves as the season progresses.
It is a most attractive bamboo that can endure dense
shade, but it can be invasive, so should be planted
in large gardens only. **USDA Zone:** Z8

■ **Tobacco plant** (*Nicotiana sylvestris* AGM)
This form of the flowering tobacco produces a
'candelabra' of highly fragrant, white blooms in
mid summer. The scent is most powerful on a still
evening. It is a choice plant for the border or as a
'dot' plant amongst bedding plants. **USDA Zone:** Z7

■ **Skimmia** (*Skimmia* x *confusa* AGM)
Skimmias are frequently grown in full sun, where the
leaves become olive-yellow and can appear sickly.
In dappled to light shade, however, the foliage is rich
green. 'Kew Green' AGM is particularly good, with
its small, white flowers that are deliciously scented.
USDA Zone: Z7

■ **Stinking hellebore** (*Helleborus foetidus* AGM)
This wonderful perennial gets its common name
because of the unpleasant smell that comes from its
foliage when crushed. To avoid the problem – don't
crush the leaves! It has pale green flowers in late
winter and is ideal for a lightly shaded part of the
garden. **USDA Zone:** Z6

Nicotiana sylvestris AGM

Skimmia x confusa 'Kew Green' AGM

Helleborus foetidus AGM

Osmunda regalis AGM

■ **The royal fern** (*Osmunda regalis* AGM)
This is a highly desirable plant for siting next to a large pond or streamside. Its lime green, prettily divided fronds first appear as copper-tinted, crooked shoots in spring, which then turn bronzy in autumn. It is a very tough plant, able to withstand cold temperatures and high winds. **USDA Zone:** Z2

■ **Viburnum** (*Viburnum* x *bodnantense*)
The deciduous *Viburnum* x *bodnantense*, which grows to around 10ft (3m) in height, produces clusters of sweet-smelling, pink flowers on its bare branches throughout winter, starting often as early as mid autumn. 'Dawn' AGM is the most popular cultivar available. **USDA Zone:** Z7

■ **Windflower, or anemone** (*Anemone blanda* 'Atrocaerulea')
This pale violet-blue, flowering plant, which grows from tubers, can also be found in white and pink. Its open, daisy-like flowers are at their best in early spring. It reaches just 6in (15cm) in height and is small enough for the fierce coastal winds to fly overhead without causing the plants any damage. **USDA Zone:** Z5

■ **Windflower, or Japanese anemone** (*Anemone* spp)
These are useful, hardy, long-lived (non-tuberous) perennials, with attractive, single flowers from late summer to late autumn. There are many varieties of *Anemone* x *hybrida*, or look for the white-flowered *A.* x *lipsiensis*. **USDA Zone:** Z6

■ **Winter aconite** (*Eranthis hyemalis* AGM)
Dappled shade is best for this gem of the winter garden, with its buttercup-yellow flowers, supported by collars of green, toothed bracts. Plants will seed themselves, to form a carpet of late winter colour. The species is good, but the vigorous cultivar 'Guinea Gold' AGM is even better. **USDA Zone:** Z5

■ **Winter hazel** (*Corylopsis* spp)
The *Corylopsis* is a delightful, underrated shrub, with an appealing late winter flowering habit. It does need an acid soil, however. The tassels are generally yellow (more yellow-green in the form *C. sinensis* var *sinensis* AGM) and delicately scented. It is related to the witch hazel (*Hamamelis*), rather than the hazelnut (*Corylus*). **USDA Zone:** Z6

Viburnum x bodnantense 'Dawn' AGM

Anemone blanda 'Atrocaerulea'

Anemone x lipsiensis

Eranthis hyemalis AGM

Corylopsis sinensis var. sinensis AGM

Chapter 17

BEST SUN-LOVING PLANTS

People move to the coast for many reasons, but one that is often high on the list of priorities is the greater number of hours of sunshine that seems to go with the territory. However, as we saw in the last chapter, bright sunlight can be the death knell for many plants. So which are the plants that thrive in full sun – by the coast?

RIGHT *Sun-lovers – including poppies – are a fixture of most coastal situations.*

Best sun-loving plants

Most gardeners look for a garden that faces the sun. In the northern hemisphere, this means a south-facing garden, whilst in the southern hemisphere it means a north-facing garden. A garden facing the sun means that we can sit and enjoy the sun's heat, without our houses casting large swathes of shade. Of course, such a garden means that we have to grow plants that also enjoy being in the sun.

During the longest days, when the sun is at its highest in the sky, your coastal garden can, if you are not careful, turn into a desert. It is easy to plant the wrong kind of plant in a sunny position. At best it will become a poor specimen and at worst you could be consigning it to an early death. And, if this happens to a number of plants, your garden could appear baked and barren.

Therefore it certainly pays to choose the plants that will be most at home in the full glare of the sun. At this point you might think of cacti and succulents, and certainly these plants are appropriate to many coastal situations. However, we are not including them in this chapter; such desert-like plants generally need poor soil, excessive dryness and copious sunshine, and the average temperate garden, even near a sunny coast, does not fulfill all of these criteria.

Fortunately there are many other plants that enjoy a position in full sun and, even when you whittle this number down to those that also tolerate wind and salty air, there is still an embarrassment of riches. Let's look at some of them.

LEFT Red hot poker lane! Kniphofia line each side of this sun-drenched spot on the Akaroa Peninsula in New Zealand.

Yucca filamentosa 'Variegata' AGM

Agapanthus 'Northern Star'

Pelargonium 'Flower Fairy White Splash'

■ **Adam's needle** (*Yucca filamentosa*)
This long-lived, stemless, evergreen perennial with sword-like leaves coming from a central rosette needs bright sunshine. In summer it produces creamy-white bell-shaped flowers in clusters on stalks. The form 'Variegata' AGM has leaves that are margined and striped yellow. **USDA Zone:** Z4

■ **African lily** (*Agapanthus* spp)
Grown for their round heads of blue trumpet-shaped flowers in summer, these plants have a distinctly exotic feel. They thrive by the sea and in full sun, but they hate root disturbance. Look for the 'Headbourne Hybrids' in colours from deep violet to pale blue. There are also white forms, and one of the deepest blues is 'Northern Star'. **USDA Zone:** Z7–9

■ **Bedding geranium** (*Pelargonium* spp)
There are hundreds of different cultivars and species available, such as the hybrid 'Flower Fairy White Splash', and they rarely disappoint. They enjoy a hot, sunny summer and tolerate drought conditions well. They flower in early summer and continue until the first frosts of autumn. **USDA Zone:** Z10

■ **Bellflower** (*Campanula* spp)
The *Campanula* genus is huge. It includes a range of biennials such as the familiar Canterbury bells, *C. medium*, available in blues and whites. There are also perennials, for example, the tall, lavender-blue *C. lactiflora*, best at the rear of the border. Another fine perennial is the dwarf *C. incurva* 'Blue Ice'. It grows to just 12in (30cm) or so, and is smothered during summer with masses of flowers with glistening blue and white tinges. **USDA Zone:** Z3–5

■ **Blazing star, or gay feather** (*Liatris* spp)
Liatris are colourful, hardy perennials, needing light, free-draining soils. They have bold spikes of feathery blooms. 'Floristan Weiss' is white, but it is more common to see lilac and purple forms, including the main species, *L. spicata*. **USDA Zone:** Z4

■ **Sea mallow** (*Lavatera maritima* AGM)
There are annual lavateras as well as the woody perennial types, such as *L. maritima,* which, as you might expect, is a good plant for the coast. It is a soft-branched shrub, which can reach up to 6ft (2m) in height. The stems are a brownish green, aging to brown before becoming a pale grey. **USDA Zone:** Z9

Agapanthus caulescens 'Blue Ice'

Liatris spicata 'Floristan Weiss'

Lavatera maritima AGM

Miscanthus sinensis 'Silberspinne'

Rudbeckia hirta 'Cappuccino'

Hemerocallis 'Children's Festival'

■ Chinese miscanthus, or eulalia
(*Miscanthus sinensis*)
With some 40 different forms, this is one grass that no garden should be without. They have an overall whitish or reddish colouring, depending on variety. The cultivar 'Silberspinne' makes an upright clump of narrow leaves, with long flower stems that are reddish at first, becoming silvery. **USDA Zone:** Z4

■ Coneflower (*Rudbeckia* spp)
There are several dozen species and cultivars of the yellow, daisy-flowered *Rudbeckia*, but some of the best for a sunny, coastal garden include forms of *Rudbeckia hirta*. Look for 'Herbstsonne' AGM (deep yellow and tall, for the back of the border) and 'Cappuccino' (deep golden-yellow tips to the petals, with a copper-brown base, giving the flowers a central dark zone). **USDA Zone:** Z3–6

■ Day lily (*Hemerocallis* spp)
There are hundreds of varieties of day lilies. The flowers do last for just one day, but they come in such profusion and over such a long period that it is not really noticeable. Most grow to 2–3ft (60–90cm) in height. 'Children's Festival' is a lovely peach, yellow and pink-flushed form. **USDA Zone:** Z3–5

■ Delphinium (*Delphinium* spp)
As well as the tall, blue-spiked perennial, this genus has become popular as summer-flowering annuals. There are also dusky pink ('Strawberry Fair') and cream ('Butterball') delphiniums available. If it is the blue forms you want, try 'Blue Butterfly' (royal blue) and 'Blue Lagoon' (mid-blue). **USDA Zone:** Z2–5

■ Dwarf mountain pine (*Pinus mugo*)
This species varies from sprawling shrubs to small trees. Most have well-spaced green needles and winter buds. The cultivar 'Gnom' reaches a height and spread of 6ft (2m). 'Mops' AGM is half this height, whilst 'Krauskopf' is half this height again at just 12–15in (30–38cm). **USDA Zone:** Z3–8

■ French marigold (*Tagetes patula*)
There are dozens of cultivars available, in shades of yellow, orange, mahogany and mixtures of the three. Most forms range from 6–12in (15–30cm) in height, with flowerheads up to 2½in (6cm) across. The African marigolds (*T. erecta*) have larger flowerheads and tend to be more shade-tolerant. **USDA Zone:** Z9

Delphinium 'Blue Lagoon'

Pinus mugo 'Gnom'

Tagetes patula 'Disco Orange'

Sedum 'Herbstfreude' AGM

Canna 'Picasso' AGM

Iris ensata 'Miyako-Oki'

■ **Ice plant, or stonecrop** (*Sedum spectabile*)
The brick-red flowers from plants of this species are hugely attractive to butterflies and bees. The best cultivar is 'Herbstfreude' AGM, known by many as 'Autumn Joy'. The flat flowerheads start rich pink, then deepen in colour. **USDA Zone:** Z4

■ **Indian shot plant** (*Canna* spp)
These tender perennials grow from thick rhizomes. Plants die down in the autumn and, if you live in a temperate or colder climate, you will need to lift the rhizomes and store them over winter. There are hundreds of varieties, most with brilliantly coloured flowers. Some also have multicoloured leaves, including 'Picasso' AGM. **USDA Zone:** Z8–10

■ **Japanese iris** (*Iris ensata* AGM)
This is one of the most impressive of irises, but it is a moisture-lover and it also dislikes limy or chalky soils. The flat flowers can be up to 8in (20cm) across, single or double, single-coloured, or blended or netted with different coloured veining. A good hybrid, though hard to find, is 'Miyako-Oki'. There are dozens of alternatives, all with very subtle differences to the flower colours. **USDA Zone:** Z4–9

■ **Knapweed, or cornflower** (*Centaurea* spp)
If you have a poor, hot, dry soil, and want plenty of bees and butterflies, then these plants are for you. *Centaurea ruthenica* has shiny, dark green, fern-like leaves and fluffy, slightly thistle-like heads of light, lemon-yellow. *C. macrocephala* is a giant example with large, fluffy, yellow flowers carried on 6ft (2m) stems from early to late summer. **USDA Zone:** Z3–6

■ **Large-flowered tickseed** (*Coreopsis grandiflora*)
All of the varieties of this yellow, daisy-flowered perennial are good for a sunny coastal garden. The flowers appear throughout summer and early autumn. Two of the best are 'Flying Saucers' and the slightly taller 'Mayfield Giant'. **USDA Zone:** Z7

■ **Love-in-a-mist** (*Nigella damascena*)
This annual blooms from early summer to mid-autumn. The straight species has pale blue flowers, but different shades have been bred over the years. Look for 'Oxford Blue' (dark blue), 'Miss Jekyll' AGM (bright blue) and *N. papillosa* 'African Bride' (white). The characteristic seedheads are attractive in their own right. **USDA Zone:** Z7

Centaurea macrocephala

Coreopsis grandiflora 'Flying Saucers'

Nigella damascena

Lupinus versicolor 'Dumpty'

Magnolia grandiflora

Aster novi-belgii 'Peter Harrison'

■ **Lupin** (*Lupinus* spp)

Lupins are grown for their early to mid summer flower spikes reaching 3–4ft (90–120cm). There are many forms and colours; some of the most attractive combine two or three colours on the individual pea-shaped flowers. *Lupinus versicolor* has a spreading dwarf habit. Flowers are blue, white or pale yellow. **USDA Zone:** Z3–4

■ **Large flowered magnolia, or bull bay**
(*Magnolia grandiflora*)

This is a superb, hardy, flowering evergreen; it starts life as a shrub, but can grow into a tree 20ft (6m) high and more. Its leaves are oval and laurel-like. The dramatic flowers are globular, thick-textured, creamy white and exude a spicy fragrance in late summer and autumn. **USDA Zone:** Z6

■ **Michaelmas daisy** (*Aster novi-belgii*)

Although these plants can suffer from mildew, asters brighten up the garden in early autumn like nothing else. There are dozens of excellent and bright cultivars. Look particularly for 'Peter Harrison' (pink with a yellow centre), 'Marie Ballard' (pale blue) and 'Winston S. Churchill' (cerise). **USDA Zone:** Z2

■ **Montbretia** (*Crocosmia* spp)

Growing from corms, these hardy perennial plants are grown for their mid- to late summer flowers. They appear on stiff stems and in a range of colours from pale orange and yellow, through to deep reds, such as the cultivar 'Lucifer' AGM. **USDA Zone:** Z7

■ **Mullein** (*Verbascum* spp)

These biennial or short-lived perennial plants are not to everyone's taste, but they do have a stately presence. They thrive in poor, dry soils and produce 5ft (1.5m) tall spikes carrying saucer-shaped flowers. 'Twilight' produces strong spikes that are cream in bud, opening to distinctive, deep apricot-pink flowers that fade to cream. **USDA Zone:** Z4–5

■ **Nepeta** (*Nepeta* spp)

There are a number of perennial nepetas. They belong to the catmint family and need a sunny spot. *N. x faassenii* AGM is the true catmint, while the cultivar 'Six Hills Giant' is twice the size, at some 3ft (90cm) in height. The slightly less hardy *N. tuberosa* grows from a rhizome and produces violet and purple flowers. **USDA Zone:** Z3–5 (*N. tuberosa* Z8)

Crocosmia 'Lucifer' AGM

Verbascum 'Twilight'

Nepeta tuberosa

Prunus 'Shosar'

Allium hollandicum AGM

Osteospermum 'Beira'

■ **Ornamental cherry** (*Prunus*)

There are hundreds of types of *Prunus*, including these Japanese flowering cherries. They are grown for their white, pink and sometimes red flowers, which can be single, semi-double and double, and are followed by the cherry fruits. *Prunus* 'Shosar' has single, blush-pink flowers. **USDA Zone:** Z2–8

■ **Ornamental onion** (*Allium* spp)

These are generally grown for their large, rounded heads of tubular flowers in various shades of purple, lilac, lavender, white, pink and blue. There are many forms to choose; *Allium hollandicum* AGM has dense purple pink flowerheads. **USDA Zone:** Z5–9

■ **Osteospermum** (*Osteospermum* spp)

If there is one perennial that could be said to be a sun-lover, it is this one. At night the daisy flowers close up, but in the sun the blooms are wide open. Flower colours vary from white and cream, through pinks, lilacs and purples. The cultivar 'Beira' has white flowers and a black 'eye'. **USDA Zone:** Z7–9

■ **Paper flower** (*Bougainvillea* spp)

In hotter countries, *Bougainvillea* covers buildings with masses of bright magenta, orange and pink flowers. In temperate countries, though, it may need winter protection, so is best grown in containers. It needs a sunny position and shelter from coastal winds. **USDA Zone:** Z9

■ **Swamp foxtail, or fountain grass** (*Pennisetum alopecuroides*)

This is a most decorative, ornamental grass. *Pennisetum* features bristly flowers, which appear in late summer and early autumn, varying from a bluish purple to pale pinkish brown. This species grows in dense clumps of bright green, narrow, arching leaves. The cultivar 'Hameln' is a low-growing form about 20in (50cm). **USDA Zone:** Z7

■ **Red hot poker** (*Kniphofia* spp)

These stately plants with tall spikes of summer flowers really give an 'architectural' quality to the garden. There are forms just 2ft (60cm) high, whilst others can reach 6ft (2m). 'Royal Standard' AGM has flowerheads graduating from yellow at the base of the 'poker', to fiery orange at the top. Other varieties have shades in the white, cream, yellow, orange and scarlet range. **USDA Zone:** Z5–7

Bougainvillea hybrid

Pennisetum alopecuroide 'Hameln'

Kniphofia 'Royal Standard' AGM

Useful resources

DETAILS OF FEATURE GARDENS

Prospect Cottage (see page 28)

Prospect Cottage, Dungeness Road, Dungeness, Romney Marsh, Kent, UK
This is a private property but can be viewed from the main road.
It is illegal to trespass.

Jardin du Soleil Lavender Farm (see page 31)

3932 Sequim Dungeness Way, Sequim, Washington 98382, USA
tel: 1-360-582-0846, toll free 1-877-527-3461
e-mail: info@jardindusoleil.com
www.jardindusoleil.com

Tresco Abbey Gardens (see page 40)

Tresco Abbey Gardens, Tresco, Isles of Scilly, TR24 0QQ, UK
tel: 01720 424108
www.tresco.co.uk

Abbotsbury Subtropical Gardens (see page 66)

Bullers Way, Abbotsbury, Nr Weymouth, Dorset, DT3 4LA, UK
tel: 01305 871387
e-mail: info@abbotsbury-tourism.co.uk
www.abbotsbury-tourism.co.uk

The Royal Botanic Gardens, Sydney (see page 69)

Royal Botanic Gardens, Mrs Macquaries Road, Sydney NSW, 2000, Australia
tel: 02-9231 8111 or weekends 02-9231 8125
www.rbgsyd.nsw.gov.au

Bodnant Gardens (see page 77)

Tal-y-Cafn, Nr Colwyn Bay, Conwy, North Wales, LL28 5RE, UK
tel: 01492 650460
e-mail: bodnantgarden@nationaltrust.org.uk
www.bodnantgarden.co.uk

Madeira Botanical Gardens (see page 90)

Madeira Botanical Garden Caminho do Meio,
Bom Sucesso 9064-251 Funchal, Madeira, Portugal
tel: 291 211200
www.madeirabotanicalgarden.com

Brookgreen Gardens (see page 108)

1931 Brookgreen Drive, Murrells Inlet, South Carolina, 29576, USA
tel: 843-235-6000
e-mail: info@brookgreen.org
www.brookgreen.org

OTHER ONLINE RESOURCES:

Australia

Garden Web: www.au.gardenweb.com
My Garden: www.mygarden.net.au

Canada

Sunshine Coast Botanical Garden Society: www.coastbotanicalgarden.org
Central Vancouver Island Botanical Garden Society: cvibgs.org

International

Mediterranean Garden Society: www.mediterraneangardensociety.org

New Zealand

NZ Gardens Online: gardens.co.nz/home.cfm
Royal New Zealand Institute of Horticulture: www.rnzih.org.nz

UK

Royal Horticultural Society: www.rhs.org.uk
Coastal gardens service & advice: www.coastalgardens.com
Coastal gardens advice: www.coastalgardens.co.uk
Gardening by the sea: www.gardeningbythesea.com

US

National Gardening Association: www.garden.org/home
San Francsco Botanical Garden: www.sfbotanicalgarden.org

FURTHER READING:

BARRON, Pattie *Make your own Mediterranean Garden* (Anness Publsihing)

COSTELLO, Lucinda *Success with Bamboos and Ornamental Grasses* (GMC Publications)

HALPIN, Anne *Seascape Gardening* (Storey Publishing)

HOBHOUSE, Penelope *Gardening* (Dorling Kindersley)

JAMES Jr, Theodore & HARALAMBOU, Harry *Seaside Gardening* (Abrams)

LATYMER, Hugo *The Mediterranean Gardener* (Frances Lincoln)

RIX, Martyn *Sub-Tropical and Dry Climate Plants* (Mitchell Beazley)

SEGALL, Barbara *Gardens by the Sea* (Frances Lincoln)

TENENBAUM, Frances *Gardening at the Shore* (Timber Press)

Photographic credits

Front cover – photographer: Jerry Harpur, design: Naila Green

All garden plans by John Bickerton

Pictures by Andrea Jones on pages: 2, 5, 6, 8–9, 10, 13, 23, 45, 58, 61, 71, 81, 93, 99, 110, 115, 121, 129, 139, 151, 159, 165, 173, 181

Part One – all pictures by John Bickerton, except:
Graham Clarke: pages 21 (bottom), 40, 41 (top), 42, 43, 46 (top and third down on right), 57 (top left)
Landcorp International: page 21 (top)
www.guernseyimages.com: page 25 (main pic)
www.morguefile.com: pages 32 (bottom left), 33 (top right), 34 (bottom left), 37 (top right and middle right), 38 (top)
Vitavia Greenhouses: page 54 (bottom right, top)
Alitex: page 54 (bottom right)
Flickr: pages 27 – tapioca22 (bottom right), 36 – David Masters (bottom, middle), 46 – Ingorr (small images, second from top)

Part Two – all pictures by John Bickerton, except:
Graham Clarke: pages 63 (bottom, middle), 65 (top left, top right and middle left), 69 (top right, middle and bottom left), 75 (top left and top middle), 76 (right), 77 (top right), 78, 83 (top right), 99 (bottom left), 106 (right), 108 (bottom left), 109 (top right)
Hozelock: pages 63 (bottom right), 87 (bottom)
Ball Colegrave: page 82 (left)
S&G Flowers: page 83 (bottom left)
Horticultural Trades Association: page 84 (bottom left)
Flickr: pages 73 – Jim Linwood (bottom right), 95 – iLoveButter (left), 96 – ewenand donabel (bottom left)

Part Three – all pictures by Graham Clarke, except:
John Bickerton: pages 116, 122, 130, 140, 152, 154 (top left), 158, 160, 166, 174, 180, 182
Eric Sawford: pages 117 (bottom right), 124 (top right), 131 (middle and bottom right), 134 (right, top and middle), 135 (top left and middle right), 136 (right, middle), 137 (top left), 141 (right, middle), 143 (left, top and middle and bottom right), 145 (bottom right), 146 (left, middle), 153 (left middle, bottom and top right), 155 (bottom left), 157 (bottom left and middle right), 161 (middle right), 170 (top left), 172 (left), 175 (top left), 176 (bottom left, top right and middle right), 177 (all, except left middle), 178 (top left and middle, bottom right and middle), 179 (left middle and bottom, top right and bottom right), 183 (top right and middle), 184 (bottom left), 185 (left middle), 187 (bottom left and top right)
Pan American Seeds: pages 153 (top left and bottom right), 154 (bottom right), 157 (middle left and top right), 175 (bottom right)
S & G Flowers: pages 153 (middle right), 154 (middle right), 157 (bottom right), D.T. Brown Seeds: pages 154 (left middle and bottom), 155 (top right), 156 middle left, middle and bottom right), 171 (middle left)
Johnson's Seeds: pages 154 (top right), 155 (middle right), 156 (top left and bottom left)
Mr Fothergill's Seeds: pages 155 (middle left), 169 (bottom right), 176 (middle left)
Ball Colegrave: pages 155 (bottom right), 156 (top right),
Fairweather's Nurseries: page 163 (middle right), 183 (middle left)
www.morguefile.com: page 176 (bottom right)
Plant World Seeds: pages 185 (top right), 186 (top left and bottom right)
Flickr: page 162 – www2.imageshop.no (bottom right)

To place an order, or to request a catalogue, contact:

GMC Publications, Castle Place, 166 High Street,
Lewes, East Sussex BN7 1XU United Kingdom
Tel: 01273 488005 Fax: 01273 402866

www.gmcbooks.com